Basic Judo

Basic Judo

E. G. Bartlett

ARCO PUBLISHING COMPANY, INC.
NEW YORK

Published 1975 by Arco Publishing Company, Inc.
219 Park Avenue South, New York, N.Y. 10003

Copyright © 1974 by E. G. Bartlett

Library of Congress Catalog Card Number 75-2707

ISBN 0-668-03790-3

Printed in the United States of America

Contents

Introduction

Judo was first introduced into Britain about the turn of the century, when Mr Barton Wright brought over a Japanese expert, Yukio Tani, who toured the music-halls, taking on all comers. He was followed by Mr S. K. Uyenishi, who made a similar tour and started teaching judo to the Army at Aldershot. Various Japanese masters followed, including Mr G. Koizumi who founded the Budokwai, one of the most famous clubs in Britain, in 1918. Mr Yukio Tani was the instructor there for many years.

Before the last war, however, judo was comparatively little known. There were approximately forty clubs in Britain, many connected with the universities, and the police had some training in the art. Since 1946, however, interest in judo has grown apace and there are now at least a thousand clubs or schools, and probably well over a hundred thousand active students, in Britain alone. A similar growth of interest has been seen in other parts of the world, especially on the continent and in the United States. Judo was included as a sport in the 1972 Olympics as well as in the 1964 games.

There is a tendency in the west to regard judo purely as a competitive sport. This is unfortunate, as it tends to suggest that its appeal is limited to those who feel themselves young enough to engage in competition. In fact, judo is much more than this. It is an art, a science, a philosophy, even a way of life. It can be practised as a means of keeping fit, or a method of self-defence, or simply out of interest, even by those who have no intention of entering championships. This book looks at all these aspects, as it is felt that the art, science and philosophy of judo will appeal even to those who consider that their competitive days are over.

To understand these deeper aspects of judo, it is necessary to look at its history, which is bound up with the history of the Japanese people. There are roughly five periods to be considered.

The Ancient period lasted from 1500 BC to AD 720. During this period, the Japanese nation came into being. There are legends of the descent of the islands and of the emperors from gods, which those who are interested in a deeper study can find in any history of Japan. It was during this period that the first emperor subjugated the hostile tribes and established the Japanese Empire. There was contact with the mainland, and aspects of Chinese and Korean culture influenced the Japanese. Confucianism came to Japan about AD 284.

The Japanese have always been adept at copying and adapting different cultures to their own ends, and there is some doubt as to whether judo did actually originate in Japan or in China. It is certainly true, however, that judo owes its more recent development to the Japanese.

In the Ancient period, the fighting arts developed as part of the essential way of life, and in addition to learning to fight with weapons, warriors were taught methods of unarmed combat. There were numerous schools and methods known by many different names, such as Yawara, Taijutsu, Kempo, Shubaku and the like. The term 'ju-jitsu' became a generic name for all these schools, 'ju' meaning 'gentle' or 'supple' and 'jitsu', 'art' or 'practice'. The methods of fighting without weapons in this early period probably have very little in common with modern judo, being more akin to sumo wrestling as far as can be ascertained. The first book ever published in Japan, the *Nihon Shoki* or *Chronicle of Japan,* contains a chapter on wrestling entitled Chikara Kurabe, which means 'superior strength'. The mere title suggests that the techniques were unlike modern judo or even ju-jitsu of a later period, since ju-jitsu and judo enable people of inferior strength to defeat those who are stronger than themselves.

There is record of a tournament held in 230 BC of Chikara Kurabe, but it was almost certainly more like sumo wrestling than judo.

From the point of view of the judo student, the next two periods in Japanese history, the Nara period (AD 720 to 793) and the Heian period (AD 794 to 1140) can be grouped together. It was during these periods that the Japanese capital was established, first at Nara and then at Heian; Buddhism and written language came to Japan, and the Fujiwara and later the samurai clans took over administrative power. Japanese wrestling was invented in this period, and Sukone Nomi compiled the system known as 'sumo' which is now very much a national sport in Japan. This is the form of wrestling in which two big men, trained from birth for the rôle, try to push each other out of the ring.

The wrestling techniques of this period were very wild and rough. There were kicks and chops such as we now associate with karate, and contests frequently ended in death. Some of the sumo throwing techniques do, however, bear a resemblance to judo throws.

The next period, known as Yoroi Kumiuchi No Jidai, is a most important one since it saw the emergence of the samurai, or warrior class. It was a feudal period in which from time to time different families would come to the fore, having deposed their rivals in the seats of power. It lasted from AD 1141 to 1526. The samurai at their best were knights with a code of honour and ethics comparable to King Arthur's Knights of the Round Table. At their worst, they were wandering thugs whose swords were for hire.

They studied the philosophy of life as well as the martial arts and the influence of their native religions, Shintoism and Buddhism, can be seen in their attitudes. Their main weapons were, of course, the sword and spear, but they also learned to fight with bow and arrow and with helmet. Before a battle between the clans, it was the custom for the champions on either side to

fight a duel, the result of which might be accepted as decisive and the battle called off. Armour was improved in this period, and as contestants had to aim for weak and exposed points, the fighting became more skilful. But the wrestling techniques remained much as they had been in the previous period.

Throughout this feudal period there was rigid class distinction between the warrior and the common man. Commoners could not bear weapons, and so for their self-defence they had to learn to fight bare-handed. This contributed to the development of techniques.

In the next period, the Tokugawa period from 1602 to 1868, outside influences were suppressed in Japan and when Hideyoshi became regent, he brought peace to the country and the armies of samurai became unnecessary.

It was during this period that the first school of ju-jitsu appeared. It was founded by Hisamori Takeuchi, who based his techniques on those of Yoroi Kumiuchi. Sumo and ju-jitsu now became definitely independent studies. A professional sumo association was set up and many judo schools apart from Takeuchi's were founded. Towards the end of this period there are said to have been over three hundred different schools and theories of ju-jitsu. The differences between the schools were often quite minor ones. A teacher would become known as a specialist in certain techniques and would build his system around them.

There was a rigid code of conduct and discipline in these schools. Often a pupil would have to enter a master's home as a servant, and prove his worthiness by serving for a long period before the master would consent to teach him. Ju-jitsu was taught under vows of secrecy and pupils had to swear never to misuse their art.

The last period to consider is the Meiji period, which extends from 1868 to the present day. The Emperor Meiji regained sovereignty from the Tokugawa clan in 1868 and a distinct decline in the martial arts followed. The wearing of swords was abolished by decree in 1871, and a policy of westernisation began in Japan.

Whilst, at the beginning of this period, ju-jitsu schools were still flourishing, these too soon began to die out and the survival of the art is largely due to Professor Jigoro Kano. Born in

1860, he became interested in ju-jitsu because he was of small stature and had learnt that the techniques enabled such as he to hold their own with bigger men. He studied under various ju-jitsu masters and selected the best techniques from them all to create his own system, which he called 'judo'. He says that 'the old style was not developed for physical education or moral and intellectual training. The latter were nothing but the incidental blessings of the former, which was exclusively devised for winning'. He found much to disapprove of in the old ju-jitsu schools. Dangerous techniques were practised, which sometimes resulted in injury. Supervision of schools had become poor, and senior pupils would bully or pick quarrels with less well advanced pupils. Some masters would present public exhibitions for money. This kind of degradation of the ancient martial arts was repugnant to Dr Kano, and it was largely for this reason that he found a new name for his system. He called it judo, the name by which it is now generally known throughout the world, and the spread of the art has largely been due to Kano and his pupils.

Kano's first practice hall was an old Buddhist temple. He founded the school in 1882, with a mat area twelve feet by eighteen feet, which is smaller than some provincial British clubs would consider adequate today. The two principles which became the basis of his system were 'maximum efficiency—minimum effort', and 'mutual aid', and these express the basis of his thought. In terms of modern mechanics, you must get a mechanical advantage from your techniques. If you overcome purely by strength, then you will not be able to overcome anyone whose strength is superior to your own. You must win with the minimum of effort. And at the basis of all your practice and effort must be the purpose of helping your partner in his studies.

Dr Kano died in 1938, after a visit to the United States to discuss bringing the Olympic Games to Japan. Not until twenty-six years later did judo become one of the sports featured at the games.

The national body of the judo organisations in Japan was the Butoku Kwai, founded in 1895. It catered not only for judo, but for the other martial arts such as kendo (sword fighting), aikido, kyudo etc. It had a membership of over three million. More recently, the International Butoku Kwai has been started by Kenshiro Abbe, who was one of the instructors in the original organisation, and when the first international judo championship was held in Tokyo in 1956 it attracted entries from twenty-one countries.

There is no single national body in any country today. In Britain, there are three main bodies: The British Judo Association, The Amateur Judo Association, and the British Judo Council, as well as minor organisations and independent teachers and schools. The European countries and the United States also have a number of national organisations. Some are linked with the Butoku Kwai; others are not. The differences between teachers and schools is largely one of emphasis. Standards are roughly similar.

In this book, we shall study first the basic principles and methods of falling; then the forty basic throws of Dr Kano's system (The Gokyo); then the basic groundwork movements, and finally three of the katas, or formal demonstrations of the art. The latter are essential to preparation for the Black Belt examination.

9

CHAPTER ONE

Basic Principles

Judo is basically an art of self-defence without weapons, based on the old ju-jitsu techniques but modified by Dr Kano to exclude the more dangerous ones.

It is practised on a mat, which takes some of the shock out of falling. The Japanese mats are made of rice straw, but substitutes sometimes used in western countries may be made of wheat straw, or rope, or of rubber. Usually these are covered by a canvas sheet stretched tight.

Students wear a special suit, called a judogi, which consists of a thick cotton jacket, trousers that come to just below the knees, and a belt or sash to wrap round the jacket and secure it, since there are no buttons on any garment to injure the student or his partner. Suits are white, and cleanliness of attire is demanded as a mark of respect to one's teacher and opponents.

The belt, or sash, is approximately nine feet long and coloured, the colour denoting the grade of the wearer. Beginners are distinguished by a red belt and it is traditional to take special care of them when practising since it is considered disgraceful to injure a beginner or anyone of a lower grade than oneself. The student stages are then: white belt (6th kyu), yellow belt (5th kyu), orange belt (4th kyu), green belt (3rd kyu), blue belt (2nd kyu), and brown belt (1st kyu). Progress to this stage would demand about two to three years' practice of several nights a week. Grading tests consist in part of contest, and in part of theory examination. The grades up to green belt do not depend on contest results, though contests are included in the tests to see how the student reacts under stress. Blue and brown belt grades, however, do depend on contest success. The general standard is to defeat three of one's own grade in order to move up to

the next, but considerable power of discretion is given to the examiner.

After reaching the highest student grade, the pupil is encouraged to go in for the black belt of the master, a process which generally takes as long again as moving up the kyu grades. Brown belt is considered to be halfway to black. The black belt is worn by masters holding the degree of first dan and above, up to fifth dan. The higher the dan the higher the degree. Sixth, seventh and eighth dans wear a red and white belt. Ninth and tenth dans wear a red belt, thus completing a full circle and coming back to the beginner's colour. Few people get that far, however, so there is no risk of confusion. Only seven men, all Japanese, have ever been awarded tenth dan and first dan is probably the limit of most European men's ambition. Only Dr Kano himself has ever held a grade higher than tenth dan. He was twelfth, and held the title 'Shihan'. A twelfth dan wears a white belt to indicate that he is above both kyu and dan grades, but it is wider than that worn by 6th kyu.

The purpose of wearing clothes when practising judo is to simulate a real life situation. If a man attacks you in the street, you will know how to use holds on his jacket or trousers which will be more effective than grasping his wrist or neck. Judo throws can, of course, be adapted to an opponent who is stripped to the waist, but in general it is assumed that an opponent will be wearing normal dress.

HOLDS

The normal holds on the opponent are taken in the following order. Stand facing him in an upright posture. With the left hand, catch his right sleeve just under the elbow from underneath, with the thumb outside and fingers in.

With the right hand, catch his left lapel, fingers outside, thumb inside, just below his left collar bone. He takes exactly the same holds on your jacket. See Figure 1.

These holds can be varied, as we shall see when studying the throws in Chapter 3, but the above is the traditional starting point.

STANCE

The basic natural stance (shizen hontai) is as follows: Stand upright with the hands hanging loosely by the sides and the feet about twelve inches apart. Relax. See Figure 2.

From this position advance the right foot about twelve inches in a natural movement forwards, and stand with the weight evenly distributed between the feet. This is known as the right natural posture (migi shizentai). If, instead, you advance the left foot, you will be taking up the left natural posture (hidari shizentai).

The other three postures are the basic defensive posture (jigo hontai), the right defensive posture (migi jigotai) and the left defensive posture (hidari jigotai). These are exactly the same as the basic natural stances except that the knees are slightly bent and the stomach is thrust forwards and downwards at an angle of 45 degrees. The angle at which the knees are bent should be 140 degrees.

Taking these defensive postures under attack will often of themselves stop throws being executed on you and will leave you ready to counter-attack.

MOVEMENT

When moving about the mat, slide the feet, keeping the sole of the foot as near the ground as possible, brushing or 'scuffing' the mat with it. If you lift your foot off the ground you are in greater danger of becoming unbalanced.

Do not bring the feet close together, but try to keep them the natural distance apart at all

2

times. Do not on any account cross the legs, unless you are attempting a throwing technique and the opponent is off balance.

Movements are generally made as follows: first, move one foot forwards, say the right; now bring the left nearly up to it, but not passing it; now move the right again; now bring the left nearly up to it, without passing it. This form of progression is known as 'tsugi ashi'.

To turn, spin on the heel or the ball of one foot whilst taking the other round it with the body in a small circle. Avoid spreading the feet too widely when doing these turns.

Diagonal movements forwards or backwards tend to be safer than ones directly forwards or directly to either side.

Remember that the natural movement is always part of the arc of a circle. Think in terms of being at the centre of a circle yourself and moving your opponent around the circumference. The application of this will be evident in the throwing techniques described in Chapter 3.

BREAKING OF BALANCE

When a man stands upright and is in the basic natural stance or in any of the stances described above, he is on balance and relatively safe. In order to throw him, or to apply any other techniques successfully, you must first upset his equilibrium.

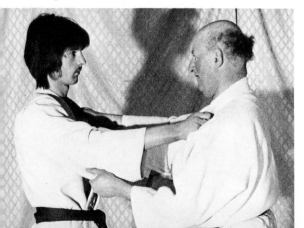

11

BASIC PRINCIPLES

To do this you must get his centre of gravity outside the rectangle that you can imagine drawn around his feet to enclose them. If you picture this rectangle, you will see that the shortest distance his centre of gravity could be moved to effect this is directly forwards. You would need to pull him by stepping back and using both your hands, so that his stomach came roughly in advance of his toes. Stepping towards him and pushing would again take his centre of gravity outside his heels and break his balance backwards.

Balance, of course, can be broken in any direction. There are 360 degrees in the circle of possibilities, but in judo we generally think of eight possible directions: directly forwards, directly backwards, to the left side, to the right side, diagonally backwards to the left, diagonally backwards to the right, diagonally forwards to the left side and diagonally forwards to the right.

Consider the nature of your own balance. When you stand upright in the natural stance your centre of gravity is roughly at the level of your stomach, and your weight acts downwards at a point midway between your feet and midway between your heels and toes. If, from this position, you are slightly unbalanced forwards, your greatest weakness is directly forwards, that is at right angles to an imaginary line drawn through your feet.

If you stand in the right natural posture, that is with your right foot advanced, then your balance could be most easily broken diagonally to your left front, that is at right angles to the imaginary line drawn through your feet. You will see this if you stand a pair of compasses up on your desk. They will fall either directly forwards or directly backwards, but always at right angles to a line drawn through the two points of support.

Breaking of balance is a vital aspect of judo. It is known as 'kuzushi' when speaking of the man who is unbalanced by the movement, and 'tsukuri' when referring to the man who does the unbalancing.

Again considering the nature of balance, you will see why it is inadvisable to bring your feet together. With such a stance your centre of gravity has only to be moved a short distance to either side to take it outside the edge of your foot, and once this has been done you are off balance in that direction.

The pull or push that breaks the opponent's balance should always be slight, just enough and no more. If you make it a big or violent, or even a sudden action, you will warn him of your intention and, if he is quick enough, he will recover. The actual throwing action, once your opponent has become unbalanced, is known as 'kake'.

Although for the purpose of description we separate the unbalancing from the throwing action, the two flow in a continuous action. There is no break or pause. To successfully throw the opponent, his balance must first be broken and this can be done either by a gentle pull or push as described above, or it may arise as a result of his own actions. When we speak of pulling or pushing, the action must be made with your whole body. Think of your arms as ropes which join your body to his. To pull him, you must first move away sufficiently far for the ropes to become taut, and then a little farther to start pulling. The arms are never stiff like rods. If they are, you use only the power of your arms, instead of the whole weight of your body.

THE PRINCIPLE OF JU

This is the principle of gentleness. The basic idea in judo is never to resist an opponent's movements, but to yield so as to turn them to his disadvantage. If, for example, he pushes you, the natural reaction is to push back. Do this, and the strongest or heaviest man will win. But if, when he pushes, you yield to his push, moving away from him, you draw him off balance in a forwards direction by bringing his centre of gravity in front of the line drawn through his toes. You can then easily throw him with such movements as 'uki otoshi', described in the chapter on throws. Similarly, when he pulls, move quickly towards him so that you are pushing him.

COURTESIES

It is traditional in the judo world to show courtesy to your instructor, to your partners, and even to the place where you practice. This is done by bowing. There are two ways, the standing bow and the kneeling bow. Both have the same purpose, to show respect, and it is a matter of custom, varying from place to place, as to which is used and when.

To make the standing salutation, the partners stand about six feet apart, heels together, hands hanging naturally at sides, and bow simultaneously from the waist. The bow is very slight, fifteen degrees from the vertical. The hands slide down the sides of the legs and the fingers are kept open. Ladies are permitted to let their hands slide down the front of their thighs when making this bow; men are not. See Figure 3.

For the kneeling salutation, partners kneel facing each other at a distance of about six feet, with the insteps close to the mat, and sit back on their heels. Their hands at this point are resting on their thighs. Together they bend forwards, placing the hands flat on the ground under their shoulders, with the fingers turned slightly inwards, and bend forwards from the waist to take the back of the head as low as the shoulders. The toes are together when making this bow. See Figure 4.

Before making either of these salutations, students should pause a moment and call to mind the purpose of the bow. It is not to be made casually, or without meaning. There must be genuine respect behind it.

The times the bow is made are as follows: when entering or leaving the hall of practice, before and after practice by the class to the instructor, before and after each individual practice to the partner or opponent, and to the place where honoured guests are seated when a display is being given for their entertainment. Always it must be made gravely and with thought of its purpose and meaning.

GENERAL BEHAVIOUR

The highest standards of behaviour are ex-

4

pected of judo students. They must never misuse their art, show off, or bully anyone inside or outside the hall of practice. They must take care not to injure lower grades when practising with them. They must be scrupulously clean and keep their finger and toe nails short. Before bowing, a judo student would adjust his jacket and belt, so that he was neatly and properly dressed, as a mark of respect to his partner.

The hall of practice is known as a 'dojo'. Professor Kano's dojo was originally a Buddhist temple, and judo students still tend to regard their dojos as near-sacred places. They are halls for study, and a student should never talk loudly or play around, or do anything that might distract or disturb those who have come there for practice. Before entering, students should put aside thoughts of rivalry or of malice towards anyone there. Co-operation and helpfulness must be the ruling spirit, so that all who come may feel they are amongst friends whose purpose it is to help them on the way to betterment. It is true that contest forms part of training, and in contest the greatest help and the greatest respect you can show to your opponent is to do your best to defeat him. But underlying this wish to defeat him at that moment, lies the long-term aim of helping him to improve his art.

METHODS OF PRACTICE

There are four methods of practice:

1. Standing Movements. This is the way in which throws are first learnt. The partner simply stands still and relaxed, and allows you to practise the throwing movement against him without offering any resistance. When he falls, he practises the breakfall. Usually partners do ten throws on each other, in turn, or rather ten repetitions of the same throw. Hundreds of thousands of repetitions are

13

needed with every movement, and to achieve these numbers more rapidly partners do not always complete the throw in this form of practice. They simply move into position, pick the opponent clear of the ground, put him down on his feet, move out, and in again. Beginners are better advised to complete the throw, however, so that the one being thrown gets practice in falling.

2. Randori. This is the name for free practice on the move, and it must not be confused with contest. Opportunities are given to try throws and resistance is varied according to skill. There is no winner or loser, so partners can relax and try out the movements learnt as standing throws when on the move.

3. Contest. This, as its name implies, is competition to see who can defeat whom. Usually a contest lasts anything from three to five minutes, or until one of the contestants gets a point. A point is given for a good clean throw. Half a point or less may be awarded for a good attempt. On the ground, a point can be won by holding for thirty seconds in a recognised holding (see Chapter 4) or for a submission. If no point is scored the referee or judges can decide the contest on style, attitude, fighting spirit and such like.

4. Kata. This is a formalised practice of throws, groundwork or self-defence, and is more fully described in later chapters.

CHAPTER TWO
Breakfalls

Breakfalling is the art of falling without hurting oneself, so that the instructions given in this chapter could also benefit people who have no intention of ever practising competitive judo.

The commonest causes of injury when people fall down in the street are letting the head flop back so that it hits first, or putting out a hand to save oneself and so damaging the wrist or arm. Knowledge of breakfalling would avoid either of these mistakes.

There are four basic breakfalls:

1. *The Backwards Breakfall* (Ushiro Ukemi)

This is best practised by taking up the crouching position shown in Figure 5, with the hands crossed in front.

Look at your belt, so that your chin is tucked in, and your head will not flop back and hit the mat. Now sit as near your heels as possible, roll back onto your shoulders, letting your feet come up, and as your shoulders hit the mat, slap the mat on either side with your whole arms, palms down, at an angle of 45 degrees from the body. See Figure 6.

Make sure your arms are at the right angle to the body. If they are too far away, you risk injuring the shoulder; if they are too close, you risk falling on them and injuring the arm. Swing the arms loosely, not tensed, and you will find that they bounce off the mat. If, when you land, your arms stay on the mat, you are holding them too tensely. The harder you slap the mat the better, since the slap absorbs part of the shock of falling.

When you can do this from a crouching position, do it from a position half way to standing, and later from a full standing position.

2. *The Side Breakfall* (Yoko Ukemi)

Stand upright. Raise the left leg straight out in front of you, resting your left hand on your left thigh. See Figure 7. Cross your right arm over your chest.

Now bend your right knee, sit as near the heel as possible and roll back as for the backwards breakfall, taking care to keep your chin tucked in and to look at your belt so that your head does not flop back and hit the mat. Let your feet come up and as your shoulders hit the mat strike it with your right arm as before at an angle of 45 degrees, palm down. See Figure 8.

This breakfall, made with the right hand, is known as 'the right side breakfall'. If you reverse the directions and do it with the left hand, it is 'the left side breakfall'.

3. *The Forward Rolling Breakfall* (Zempo Kaiten Ukemi)

From the normal standing position, advance the right foot, bend the knee, and place both hands on the ground, fingers pointing inwards. See Figure 9.

From this position, push yourself off with your left leg, roll directly forwards, head over heels, and land on your back in the side breakfall position, slapping the mat with your left hand at the same angle as in the side breakfall. See Figure 10.

This is known as 'the right rolling breakfall'. If you reverse the directions by putting your left leg forwards, pushing off with your right leg and slapping with your right hand, you are doing 'the left rolling breakfall'. Both are needed, of course, and both should be practised.

4. *The Front Breakfall* (Mae Ukemi)

This is little used to day and is a survival of the ju-jitsu days when it was permissible to throw the opponent forwards onto his face. This is no longer allowed, so that the only use of the

5

7 8

6

front breakfall is where a rolling breakfall would be the normal action but you are too close to the ground to do it.

In the front breakfall, you land on your forearms and hands, which are turned inwards in much the same position as for the kneeling bow, and on the toes of your feet. Your body is straight and off the mat, so that neither your nose, your stomach, nor your knees hit the mat. It is best practised first by kneeling down, bending forwards and striking the mat with the forearms in the right position. When you can do that, combine it with shooting out the legs, spreading them and coming up on the toes. From here, move on to simply falling directly forwards, and then at a later stage giving a little jump into it. Figure 11 clearly illustrates the position of landing.

These breakfalls are used when landing from any of the throws described in the next chapter, and the student should gain confidence in doing them before being thrown. Initially, it is best if he is only thrown by a teacher, who can put him down gently, until he has gained confidence in breakfalling. He should not do 'randori', or free practice, until he is proficient in all the breakfalls on either side.

10

CHAPTER THREE
The Gokyo

From the many existing throws and variations of throws, the Kodokan have selected forty basic ones and arranged them into five sets, eight in each set. To this course of instruction they have given the name 'The Gokyo'. These sets, it should be pointed out, do not get progressively harder; in fact, the first throw of the first set needs great skill and perfect timing to perform. The order is simply that in which the Kodokan have chosen to arrange them.

Although the throw is described on the right-hand side in each case, and leads to a left-hand side breakfall or a right rolling breakfall, every throw can be done on either side and should be practised on both left and right, simply by reversing the directions.

SET ONE

1. *Sweeping an Advancing Foot* (De Ashi Barai)

The opportunity for this occurs when you are both standing in the normal posture with the normal holds, and the opponent steps forwards with his right foot. You can lead him to do this usually with a gentle pull on his right sleeve as you step back with your right foot. Note that your whole body must move back when you step away from him, so that it is your whole body weight pulling him and not just the strength of your arm. As he steps forwards and is about to transfer his weight onto the foot he puts forward, turn your left foot and sweep his foot across his body from his right to his left, at the same time pulling down on his sleeve with your left hand and giving a little lift with your right hand on his lapel. See Figure 12.

The point of contact with his foot is just below the ankle. If you time your movement just as the transfer of weight is taking place,

he will be swept clean off the ground. At this stage, let go with your right hand but retain the hold on his sleeve with your left hand and, as he lands, pull up slightly to assist his breakfall and make his landing a little softer. This care of one's partner should be practised in all throws, particularly if you are practising with someone less experienced than yourself. The effect of the throw is as seen in Figure 13.

2. *Knee Wheel* (Hiza Guruma)

This is usually done when the partner has his right foot to the rear and is about to bring it forwards. Let him stand in that position for you to practise. Now imagine a line drawn through his feet and extended beyond them. Step in with your right foot, so that it is on this line with the toes pointing up the line towards your partner. With both hands tilt him directly forwards over his toes. Raise your left leg and place the sole of the foot on the outside of his right knee. See Figure 14.

Turn your body and with both hands throw him over your foot. The hands lift him initially and then pull down as he loses balance and falls. See Figure 15.

3. *Propping Drawing Ankle Throw* (Sasae Tsurikomi Ashi)

Step back diagonally to your right rear with your right foot, turning your body and foot so that the foot points towards the partner at a 45 degree angle. With both hands lift and pull your partner so that he is balanced on his toes and wants to step forwards with his right foot to regain his balance. See Figure 16.

Before he can step forwards, apply the sole of your left foot to the front of his shin just above the instep. Continue turning your body away from him, pulling with your hands, so that he

2

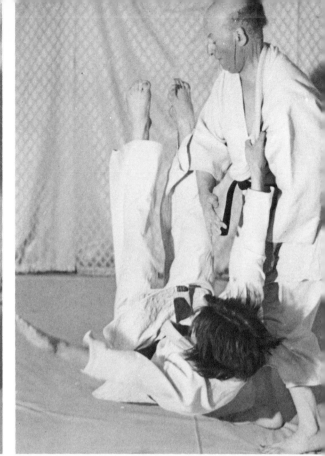

14 15

13

trips over your outstretched foot. As he falls, pull down with your left hand to encourage the falling motion and, of course, lift slightly as he lands to enable him to breakfall. See Figure 17.

4. *Floating Loin Hip Throw* (Uki Goshi)

Step in with your right foot to a point midway between his feet, turning your body so that your right side is against his chest and stomach. At the same time give a lift pull with your left hand and let go with your right hand and slide it around his back on the level of his belt. This hand and the pull of your left holds him tight against your side. Bend your knees slightly as you move in. See Figure 18.

Now throw by straightening your knees to bring him off the ground and continuing to turn. Turn your head and let your whole body follow. See Figure 19.

He should land in front of you and directly across your feet, though not on them, of course.

5. *Major Outer Reaping Throw* (O Soto Gari)

Your partner's feet are on a line. Step in with your left foot onto the same line and place it just outside his right. With your right hand push up over his shoulder and down towards his right heel. With your left hand push down towards his right heel. Take your head and your whole body in, so that you are looking over his right shoulder at the ground and your right shoulder is pushing against him, thus using the weight of your body as well as your hands. The effect of all these actions is to pin the partner on his right heel. See Figure 20.

Now swing your right leg through the gap between your left and his legs and use it to sweep away his right leg on which he is supported. The action should be a sweeping one, not a hook or a kick. The point of contact is between the back of your right thigh and the back of his. Turn slightly to your left as you throw. See Figure 21.

6. *Major Hip Throw* (O Goshi)

Lift and pull slightly with both hands so that the partner comes onto his toes. This is a rocking motion and very gentle, or he will see what is coming and resist. Step in with your right foot to just inside his right. Take your right hand behind his back and place it on his right shoulder blade as you turn your back to him. Bring your left foot back around in a small circle and place it just inside his left. In this position both your

knees should be bent and your right hip should project beyond his just enough for you to pick him up on it when you straighten your knees. See Figure 22.

Throw by continuing to turn, bringing him over your hip and down in front of you. See Figure 23.

7. *Major Inner Reaping* (O Uchi Gari)

Step in towards him, with your left foot, turning your right side to him. The foot is placed pointing across his body towards his right and about a foot in front of his toes. Pull forwards with your left hand and with your right push over his shoulder and down, so as to pin his weight on his left heel. See Figure 24.

Insert your right leg between his and use it to sweep away his left, on which his weight is pinned. The movement is a circular one. Take his leg out slightly and then forwards. Whereas in all the throws described so far the partner falls with a left side breakfall, in this throw he does the backwards breakfall, unless you retain the hold on his right sleeve, in which case he might be turned into a left side breakfall. See Figure 25 for the throw.

8. *Shoulder Throw* (Seoi Nage)

Lift and pull his right arm with your left, at the same time stepping in with your right foot to just inside his right and turning on it. As you turn your back to him bring your left foot back inside his left, with your heels on the same line as his toes, and at the same time thrust your right shoulder under his right armpit. With your right hand let go the hold on his lapel as you start to move in and, instead, catch his jacket high up on the right shoulder. Bend your knees as you move in. See Figure 26.

To throw, straighten your knees to lift him on your back. Continue turning and throw him over your right shoulder to the ground. The action is like having a sack on your shoulder and shrugging it off. You do not take him directly over and onto his head, but rather around you and certainly onto his back. See Figure 27.

SET TWO

1. *Minor Outer Reaping Throw* (Ko Soto Gari)

Your partner's feet are on a line. Step first to his right side with your left foot and then in with

26 27

25

your right foot, so that your right toes are pointing towards him and on the same line as his feet. Your body is at right angles to his, facing towards him, on his right side. With your left hand pull down, breaking his balance to his rear, and with your right hand push up, over and down, reinforcing this breaking of balance. Place the sole of your left foot behind his right heel and push it forwards. The position and the effect of the throw are seen in Figures 28 and 29.

An opportunity often occurs for this throw when the partner has moved into position for a hip or shoulder throw, and having failed to bring it off is moving back out again. As he is bringing his right foot back out his right side is momentarily towards you, and if you are quick enough you can use this throw as a counter throw.

2. *Minor Inner Reaping Throw* (Ko Uchi Gari)

The opportunity for this occurs when your partner steps directly forwards with his right foot. Take your left foot back and around behind you in a small circle, and place it about twelve inches in front of his left foot, toes pointing across his body from his left to his right. Turn your body as you do this, so that your left shoulder moving away, combined with the resultant pull on his right sleeve with your left hand, causes him to step forwards with his right foot. As he does so, turn your right foot so that you can put the sole in contact with his right heel from behind. See Figure 30.

Now, as he is about to put his weight on his right foot, push it just a little forwards with your right from behind. Pull forwards with your left hand and with your right push up, over his shoulder, and down towards his right rear. The effect is as if he had stepped on a banana skin. His right foot is taken from under him and he should leave the ground completely. See Figure 31.

As with all the foot throws, perfect timing of the push with your foot, co-ordinated with the pull and push, is required. Timing and co-ordination of this order come only with long practice, and judo masters tend to have one or two pet throws for which they become famous. Those who select this kind of throw may work on it for ten years or so to perfect their timing.

3. *Hip Wheel* (Koshi Guruma)

The partner's balance is broken directly for-wards for this hip throw. Give a lift and pull with your left hand, and a pull with your right hand to tilt him onto his toes. Step in with your right foot to just inside his right, turning on it and taking your left foot back and inside his. Let go with your right hand and put your arm round the back of his neck to tilt him further forwards. Your right hip must be taken right through and past him. Continue turning, by swivelling on your left foot and bringing your right forwards and round, so that you have the partner across your back. See Figure 32.

Your knees are bent when making the above movements, so that you can come in under him. Straighten your knees to lift him clear of the ground and throw by continuing to turn and bringing him over your back. Let go the hold round his neck as he falls. See Figure 33.

It is most important that the pull on his right sleeve with your left hand should be maintained strongly as a continuous movement.

4. *Resisting Hip Throw* (Tsurikomi Goshi)

Break his balance directly forwards with a lift pull on his right sleeve with your left hand. Step in with your right foot to just inside his right, turning on the foot to bring your left in to just inside his left. Bend your knees much more than for the earlier hip throws, so that your hips are in contact with the front of his thighs. Thrust your right elbow under his left armpit and use it to lift him more strongly. See Figure 34.

Straighten your knees to lift him clear of the ground and thrust your hips backwards to throw, while continuing to turn. See Figure 35.

This throw can also be made as a follow-on to a major hip throw that has failed to come off. When you are in position for the major hip throw, simply bend your knees more so that you drop under him into position for this throw. A variation to the throw is to catch his left sleeve from the outside at the elbow joint with your right hand and to lift this up in the air, instead of thrusting the right elbow under his left armpit. This is effective against any opponent who maintains stiff arms—something no experienced judo men are likely to do.

5. *Double Ankle Sweep* (Okuri Ashi Barai)

The opportunity for this throw occurs when the partner brings his feet together. Step in with your left foot towards him and just outside his

32   34 35

right foot. Turn your body at the same time and take your right foot back, pulling on his left lapel with your right hand and lifting slightly. The effect of this is to make him advance his left foot. See Figure 36.

With your left hand push towards his body and continue your turn. This will lead him to move his right foot up to his left. As he does so, turn your left foot and place the sole against the outside of his right foot, pushing it into his left. Lift with your right hand and pull down with your left. These actions must be simultaneous and timed to coincide with his movement of his right foot. The effect is to sweep him clean off the ground. See Figure 37.

With opponents who are incautious enough to bring their feet close together, or who skip around, this throw can be done simply by sweeping the foot they are bringing up into the other and pulling down with the hand on that side and lifting with the hand on the other side. Few experienced men will make these skipping movements of themselves, however, or bring their feet too close together, and you have to try and make them as described above. An effective variation of the right-hand lift is to let go the lapel and lift under the left armpit. It is very strong and almost invariably makes the opponent bring his right foot up close to his left.

6. *Body Drop* (Tai Otoshi)

Take your left foot back around you in a small circle and place it to point in the same direction as the partner's toes and about a foot in front of his left foot. Turn your body at the same time and pull strongly on his right sleeve with your left hand. The pull is with the whole of your body turning, not just with the hand alone. With your right hand, lift and bring forwards so that the partner's weight is brought onto his right toes. At this stage, bring your right leg across and place the toes on the ground just outside his right foot. Your right leg now blocks his advance. See Figure 38.

The point of contact between your leg and the front of his shin must be low down. If you are too high up he will block your attempt by bending his right knee. There must be no body contact between you and there should be a straight line down your right side from heel to head. To throw, simply continue to turn and he

will fall over your outstretched leg. Maintain a strong pull with your left hand from start to finish of this movement. See Figure 39.

7. *Sweeping Hip Throw* (Harai Goshi)

Break the partner's balance directly forwards with a lift pull on his right sleeve with your left hand and a pull on his lapel with your right. Step in with your right foot to just inside his right, turning on it to take your left back to just inside his left. This is as for the hip throws previously described. With your right hand, let go his lapel and take it behind his back onto his right shoulder blade. Now sway your weight onto your left leg so that you can raise the right leg off the ground. See Figure 40.

Turn and with your outstretched right leg sweep his right leg backwards and up, throwing him down in front of you. Note that the sweep must be made with the back of your thigh against his thigh. It must not be a hook at the level of the shin or ankle. See Figure 41.

8. *Inner Thigh* (Uchi Mata)

Pull gently on his left lapel with your right hand to lead him to advance his left foot. As he does so, step in with your left to a point about midway between his legs. Pull his right sleeve towards your left side. Insert your right leg between his legs so that you can use it to sweep his left thigh from the inside. See Figure 42.

Now, as he is about to transfer his weight from his right leg to his left, sweep his left upwards with your right thigh from the inside and turn him off your leg with the combined action of both your hands. See Figure 43.

The above description of the throw is as it is usually performed today. It can also be performed more clearly, however, as a foot throw in the following manner. Step back and around with your left foot to a point just outside his left and on the same line, turning your body as you do so. Break his balance forwards with a pull on his right sleeve with your left hand and by lifting and turning your right wrist forwards. This balances him on his toes. Insert your right leg between his as previously described. See Figure 44.

Now, continue to turn to your left, lift his left leg from inside his thigh with your right, or a little lower down than the thigh, pull forwards and downwards with your left hand and turn

him off your outstretched right leg with the combined action of both your hands. See Figure 45.

SET THREE

1. *Minor Outer Hook* (Ko Soto Gake)

With your right foot, step forwards to a point midway between your partner's legs. With your left hand push down towards his right heel. Take your right hand, holding his lapel up and over his shoulder so that your wrist rests on his shoulder, and continue the movement down to his rear. This has the effect of pinning him on his heels. See Figure 46.

With your left leg, hook his right behind the knee, from outside and pull it forwards as your hands continue to push him backwards and down. See Figure 47.

It is essential that your hands definitely pin him on his heels, not simply push back, otherwise he will step back and so escape.

2. *Lifting Hip Throw* (Tsuri Goshi)

Pull with your left hand in a lift pull to break the partner's balance to the front. Step in with your right foot to just inside his right and turn on it, taking your left back to just inside his left. With your right hand let go his lapel, pass it over his left arm and grasp his belt at the back. See Figure 48.

You should bend your knees slightly when executing the above movements. Now straighten your knees and with a strong pull with both hands bring his body into tight contact with yours. Turn and throw him over your hip. See Figure 49.

If the partner is much shorter than you, you can pass your right arm over his left shoulder to grasp the belt. A strong lift on the belt then brings him up onto your hips. It is not permissible to hold the belt continuously in contest, but it is permitted to catch it for the performance of this throw.

3. *Side Drop* (Yoko Otoshi)

By pulling down on the partner's right sleeve with your left hand and lifting on his lapel with your right hand, break his balance directly to his right side. Slide your left foot in to just outside his right ankle and fall onto your own left side. See Figure 50.

Pull him to your left with both hands and he will fall to your left side with his body almost parallel with yours. See Figure 51.

It is essential to use your hand movements to turn your partner onto his back when performing this throw. Not only is it forbidden by the rules to bring him down onto his right shoulder, but it will break his right collar bone if you do. So be very careful. It is for this reason that this throw and others listed at the end of this chapter are banned to grades below brown belt.

4. *Leg Wheel* (Ashi Guruma)

This is usually performed when the partner has his right leg to the rear and is about to bring it forwards. Step back and around with your left foot, placing it on a line drawn through your opponent's feet, with the toes pointing in the same direction as his and just outside his left foot. With both hands tilt him onto his toes, breaking his balance at right angles to the line drawn through his feet and in a forwards direction. Stretch out your right leg and place it in front of his, so that it blocks his advance, above the knee of his left leg and below the knee of his right leg. Your right toes are not on the ground. See Figure 52.

Bend forwards slightly from the hips to tilt him still further over his toes and, as he loses balance, turn to your left. Then, with the action of your hands and the turning of your body, throw him forwards over your outstretched right leg. See Figure 53.

Note particularly that your right leg simply blocks his advance. It does not sweep his legs back. You will find that the throw can almost be performed without the use of the leg. He is tilted onto his toes and will fall by your body turn alone if he does not save himself by advancing his right foot. Your leg stretched across his stops him making this movement, which would save him.

5. *Spring Hip Throw* (Hane Goshi)

Break your partner's balance to the front with a lift pull on his right sleeve with your left hand and a pull with your right hand. Step in with your left foot to a point midway between his legs. Raise your right leg and, bending it at the knee, place it across the front of his legs with your right knee projecting beyond his right knee. Let go with your right hand and pass it round his back. With both hands hold his body tight against your right side and on his toes. See Figure 54.

46 47   45

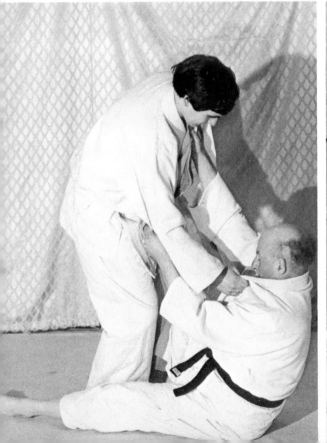

54 55

53

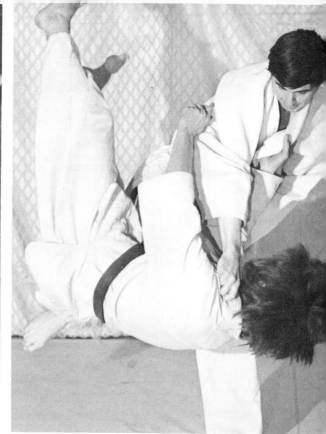

Holding him tight against you, sway your weight to your left, lifting him clear of the ground, and turn, bringing him over your right hip and down. See Figure 55.

Your bent right leg helps to lift him.

6. *Sweeping Drawing Ankle* (Harai Tsurikomi Ashi)

Step back diagonally to your right rear with your right foot, turning it to point towards the opponent at an angle of 45 degrees. Pull forwards and upwards with your left hand on his right sleeve, and lift and pull with your right hand on his left lapel. The effect is to break his balance towards his right front corner, so that he wants to step forwards with his right foot to regain his balance. Up to this point the throw is exactly the same as the Propping Drawing Ankle Throw, described in Set One, no. 3. See Figure 56.

Continue turning and pulling forwards with your left hand, pulling in a natural circle and not at a tangent towards your own body. This will lead him to actually take the step forwards with his right foot in order to regain his balance. As he is in the middle of the step and about to transfer his weight, push his right leg back with the sole of your outstretched left foot. See Figure 57.

Do not sweep too high. Think of making contact at the bottom of his shin with the little toe edge of your left foot making contact with the top of his right foot.

7. *Stomach Throw* (Tomoe Nage)

With both hands lift and pull the partner so that he is tilted onto his toes. Slide your left foot in between his legs. Raise your right leg and place the sole of your foot about two inches below his navel, falling backwards onto your back as you do so. Your falling weight brings him forwards over you. See Figure 58.

Straighten your right leg and pull with both hands, and you will throw him directly over your head onto his back. He will land with the right rolling breakfall. See Figure 59.

This type of throw, in which you fall down yourself in order to throw your opponent, is known as a 'sacrifice throw'. Of them all, it is the only one allowed in beginner's contests, as it is the least dangerous. The disadvantage of this type of throw is, of course, that if it fails you have sacrificed your own standing position, and the opponent is likely to fall on top of you and start groundwork. See Chapters 4, 5 and 6. Judo students tend to specialise in standing techniques or groundwork, so if you are not very good on the ground avoid resorting to sacrifice throws.

8. *Shoulder Wheel* (Kata Guruma)

Pull on your partner's right sleeve with your left hand so that he advances his right foot. As he does so, step in with your right foot between his legs. Bend your knees and lower your body. Put your right hand between his legs and grasp his trousers behind his right thigh. Put the back of your head against his right side at about his belt level. As you are doing this, change your left hand hold on his right sleeve from an outside grip to an inside grip and pull it towards your left chest. See Figure 60.

Now bring your left foot closer to your right one, at the same time straightening your legs and so lifting your partner onto your shoulders. The position is similar to what is popularly called the 'fireman's lift'. Throw him over your head so that he falls on his back obliquely to your left front corner. See Figure 61.

SET FOUR

1. *Corner Throw* (Sumi Gaeshi)

This type of throw is performed from the defensive, rather crouching posture that some opponents adopt. It has tended to die out with the more upright posture that is in fashion today. However, with both of you bending forwards slightly and knees bent, let go with your right hand and place it behind the opponent's back, under his left armpit. Rest your right hand on his right shoulder blade if possible. With your left hand pull his right sleeve as tightly as you can against your left side. From this position place your left foot midway between his legs and to the rear of his heels. Fall on your back, raising your right leg and placing the instep against the inside of the knee of his left leg. See Figure 62.

With your right leg, lift his left upwards and towards your head. With your left hand pull down and with your right hand lift, and he will be thrown over your head. All these movements, though described separately, have, of course to be synchronised in practice. The opponent lands with a right rolling breakfall. See Figure 63.

58 59

57

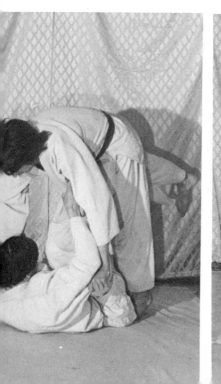
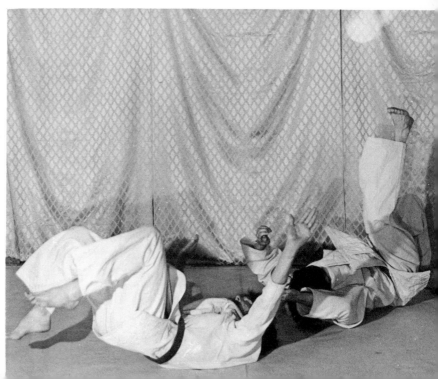

60

62 63

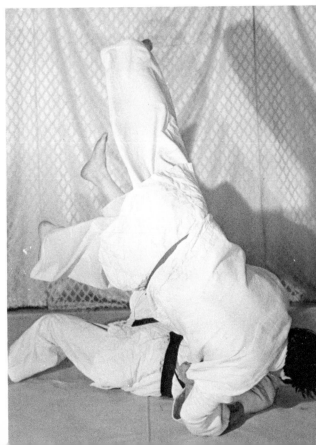

2. *Valley Drop* (Tani Otoshi)

At first, this looks very similar to the Side Drop described in Set Three, no. 3. The difference is largely one of direction of throwing, which depends on the direction in which the opponent's balance is broken.

Advance your left foot deeply outside his right, the knee of your left leg being about the position of his right ankle. Put your right hand under his left armpit. With your left hand pull his right sleeve to your left side. Fall on your left side. See Figure 64.

With the lift of your right hand and the pull of your left, combined with your falling weight, throw him over your outstretched left leg behind your left shoulder. See Figure 65.

3. *Outer Winding Spring Throw* (Hane Maki Komi)

This is a combination of Soto Makikomi (no. 7 of this set), and Hane Goshi (no. 5 of Set Three). Lift pull with your left and right hands to bring him onto his toes. Step in with your left foot to a position midway between his, turning your right side to him. Bend your right leg and put it across his legs. Now, holding him tight against you with your left hand pull, take your right arm over his right. See Figure 66.

Continue turning, put your right hand on the ground and roll onto your right side. Your partner is whipped over your body and lands beside you. See Figure 67.

4. *Scooping Throw* (Sukui Nage)

Let go his sleeve with your left hand and grasp his left lapel at about the position that your right hand normally grasps it. Step to his right side so that you are facing him, your body at right angles to his, your left foot behind him and your right foot in front. Bend your knees. With your right hand grasp either the back of his jacket or his belt, thrusting your hand between his legs to do so. See Figure 68.

Push back against his chest with your left forearm and pull forwards with your right hand, at the same time straightening your knees and thrusting your stomach under your partner. You will be able to lift him clear of the ground. See Figure 69.

Now simply drop him onto his back, or throw him in the direction of his head so that he falls onto his back.

5. *Changing Hip Throw* (Utsuri Goshi)

This is a counter throw. Your partner attempts any of the hip throws on you, such as O Goshi (Set One, no. 6), or Uki Goshi (Set One, no. 4). Bend your knees and thrust your stomach forwards to block his throw. With your left arm grasp him along the line of his belt at the rear and, with your right elbow on your right hip, use your right hand to push him backwards. Straighten your knees and you will be able to lift him clear of the ground and swing his legs to his rear. See Figure 70.

At the moment when he has been swung back, slip your left hip under him by stepping forwards with your left foot. You will then be able to perform the hip throw on him on the opposite side to normal by simply turning and pulling down with your right hand. See Figure 71.

6. *Major Wheel* (O Guruma)

Step back and around with your left foot to a position just inside his left foot, on the same line

66

68 69

72 73 71

and facing the same way. With your left hand break the opponent's balance forwards. With your right hand bring him close to your right side and onto your right hip. Stretch out your right leg across the front of his legs. See Figure 72.

Continue turning to your left and, by swinging your right leg back and up, lift him off the mat and over your hip. See Figure 73.

This resembles the Leg Wheel (Ashi Guruma: Set Three, no. 4), but the partner is thrown over your hip rather than just your leg, and his balance is broken more to his left front corner than directly forwards with the pull of your right hand.

7. *Outer Winding Throw* (Soto Maki Komi)

Lift and pull on his right sleeve with your left hand. Take your left foot back and around and place it just in front of his left foot. Let go with your right hand and take your right arm over his right arm. Stretch out your right leg and place the foot just outside his right foot to block his advance. Now, with the combined pull of your left hand and the push of your right upper arm, trap his right arm under your right armpit. See Figure 74.

Turn your body to your left, put your right hand on the ground, and fall on your right side. The opponent is wound over your body and falls beside you. See Figure 75.

8. *Floating Drop* (Uki Otoshi)

Step back diagonally with your right foot and point the toes at an angle of 45 degrees towards the partner. With your right hand, lift to bring him onto his toes. With your left, lift and pull so that he wants to step forwards with his right foot to regain his balance. See Figure 76.

At the point where he wants to step forwards, but before he does so, pull down with your left hand and lift with your right simultaneously. The effect is to turn him in a large circle towards his right front. See Figure 77.

SET FIVE

1. *Major Outer Wheel* (O Soto Guruma)

Step in with your left foot onto the same line as the partner's feet and just outside his right foot. With your left hand push down towards his right heel. With your right hand, push up and over his shoulder and then down his back, resting your right wrist bent on his left shoulder. The effect of these moves is to pin him on both heels, with his balance broken directly to his rear. Swing your right leg through the gap between your left and his right, and stretch it out so that it is above his right knee and below his left. See Figure 78.

Turn left and use your outstretched right leg to sweep both of his away. See Figure 79.

The throw is not unlike O Soto Gari (Set One, no. 5), except that as you are sweeping both his legs away it is rather more violent.

2. *Floating Throw* (Uki Waza)

Pull the partner forwards with both hands so that his balance is broken directly forwards. Stretch out your left leg to your left and fall on your left side, bringing your left hand to your left side as you do so and pushing with your right hand so as to throw the partner over your outstretched left leg. See Figures 80 and 81.

Your partner should land behind you slightly and to your left side. He does a right forwards rolling breakfall.

3. *Side Separation* (Yoko Wakare)

Lift pull with both hands to break your partner's balance directly forwards. Turn your right side towards him and slide your left foot widely to his right, at the same time dropping onto your left side immediately in front of him. See Figure 82.

Slide your right foot through also as you are falling, so that your two feet block his advance. As you fall, you pull down strongly with both hands and as his weight is tilted over his toes he somersaults forwards over your waist and lands on his back at approximately right angles to your body. See Figure 83.

This particular throw, although banned to lower grades, is used as a counter-throw to such throws as O Goshi (Set One, no. 6), by stepping quickly round in front of the opponent and falling.

4. *Side Wheel* (Yoko Guruma)

Step in with your left foot to behind your partner's right, turning your body to face his side. Your feet are evenly spaced, one in front and one behind him, and you are facing his right side, at right angles to it. With both arms, clasp him around the waist, at the level of his belt. See Figure 84.

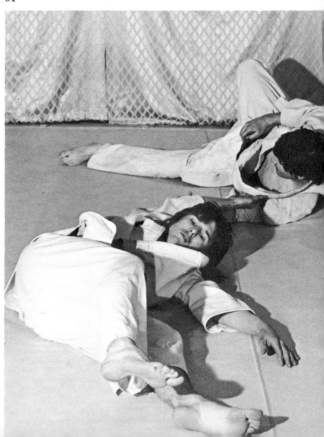

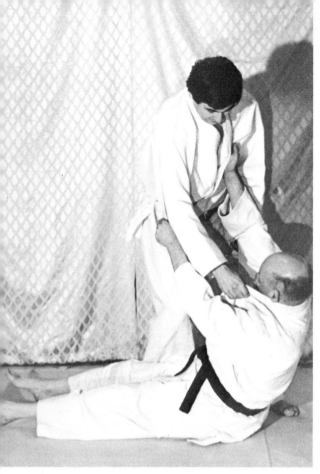

84 85

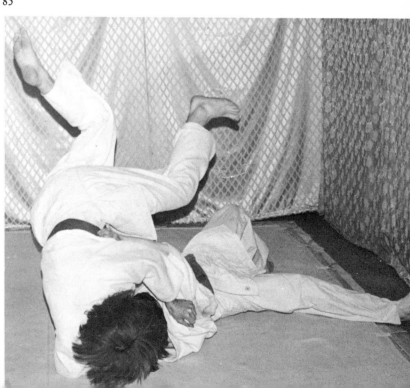

86

88 89

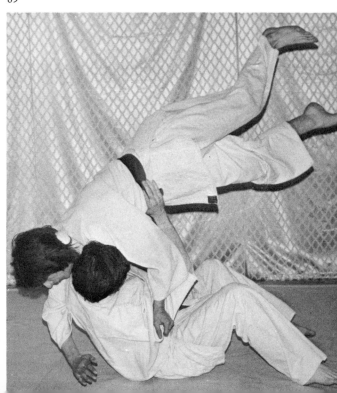

This is the kind of position from which you would do the Changing Hip Throw (Set Four, no. 5), or the Rear Throw (no. 6 of this set). To counter any attempt at these, the partner will lean forwards when you take up your position. As he does so, slide your right foot deeply between his and fall on your back, rolling onto your left side. See Figure 85.

Your partner will land just behind your left shoulder with a forwards rolling breakfall.

5. Rear Loin (Ushiro Goshi)

This is a counter-throw to an attempt at one of the hip throws. Let the partner move in for Uki Goshi (Set One, no. 4). As he comes in, bend your knees to lower your hips and clasp him around the waist at belt level with both hands. Lean backwards and thrust your stomach forwards so that it is below his hips, and you can lift him on it. See Figure 86.

By straightening your knees whilst holding him tight and thrusting your stomach forwards, lift him clear of the mat, swinging his legs forwards so that he levels out. At the peak of your lift, walk backwards from under him so that he falls onto his back. See Figure 87.

It is permissible to use the left knee to assist your lift.

90

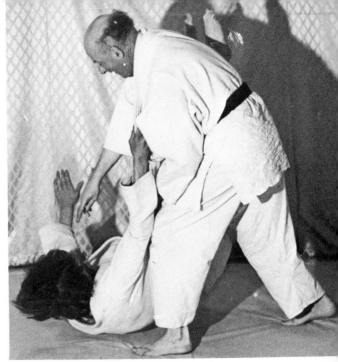

91

6. Rear Throw (Ura Nage)

Step in to your partner's right side, your left foot behind him, your right foot in front of him, your body at right angles to his and facing him. Catch him around the waist with your knees bent, your left arm encircling the line of his belt, and your right hand in his stomach. See Figure 88.

Bend backwards as you straighten your knees so that you lift him clear of the mat. At this moment throw yourself backwards onto your back and hurl him over your left shoulder to your rear. See Figure 89.

This is rather a dangerous technique. Practise it with care, and do not land the partner on his head but let him go with your left arm so that he can do a rolling breakfall.

7. Corner Drop (Sumi Otoshi)

Step in with your left foot to just outside his right, bending your knees as you do so. With your left hand push towards his right heel. With your right hand, push up over his left shoulder and down towards his right heel. The effect of this is to pin him on his right heel. See Figure 90.

Now push with your right hand and pull with your left, and you will turn him onto his back, probably getting both his feet off the ground but certainly his left. This is not an easy throw as it is executed largely with the hands alone. It is

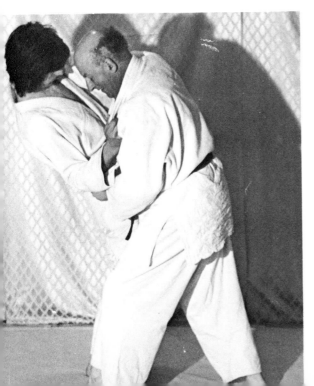

45

THE GOKYO

similar to Uki Otoshi (Set Four, no. 8), the only difference being the direction of throw. See Figure 91.

8. *Side Body Drop* (Yoko Gake)

Pull with your left hand so that the partner will advance his right foot. As he does so, apply the sole of your left foot to the side of his right and fall backwards and to your left side. See Figure 92.

As you are going down, keep a strong pull going with your left hand and with your right push him so as to turn him onto his back. Sweep his right ankle across his body from his right to his left. He will land on his back, almost parallel to your body. See Figure 93.

These forty techniques cover most of the basic throws in judo today. It will be found that the others are really just variations on these, although one authority says that there are over six hundred listed throws. As has been said, these techniques can be applied to right or left side, giving eighty ways in all of throwing the partner.

Because of their dangerous nature, the following are discouraged below the grade of brown belt, if not actually forbidden. In some dojos they would be forbidden at any grade:

Set Three, no. 3 (Yoko Otoshi)
Set Four, no. 1 (Sumi Gaeshi)
Set Four, no. 2 (Tani Otoshi)
Set Four, no. 3 (Hane Maki Komi)
Set Four, no. 7 (Soto Maki Komi)
Set Five, no. 2 (Uki Waza)
Set Five, no. 3 (Yoko Wakare)
Set Five, no. 4 (Yoko Guruma)
Set Five, no. 6 (Ura Nage)
Set Five, no. 8 (Yoko Gake)

If you practise these throws, then, take special care and only do so under the supervision of a master.

All the techniques in this and the three following chapters should be learnt by any student who is interested in contest. Judoka (judo students) tend to specialise in the one or two techniques that they find suit them best, and in the course of time you will no doubt develop your own 'pet throws'.

The throws should be practised first as standing movements, then by simply doing the movement without throwing (an exercise called 'batsukari'), then in randori, or free practice, to gain experience in applying them on the move. Finally, they should be tried in contest.

Even for those students who are not primarily interested in contest, practice of these throws will constitute a very fine exercise. Consider, for example, the throw Kata Guruma (Set Three, no. 8). The action of bending the knees and lifting the partner onto one's shoulders whilst straightening them, bears a distinct resemblance to the body-builder's exercise in which he does a deep knees bend with a weight across his shoulders. The same muscles are used and developed by this exercise.

The throws also have their application in self-defence, of course, and we shall see in Chapter 9 how some of them are applied to this end.

Speed and timing are the secrets of success in throwing. The opponent is only off balance for a fraction of a second. You must see the moment coming and apply your throw at that precise instant. The time to attack is when he is breathing in, if possible. By constant practice of randori you will develop a kind of sixth sense that tells you what the other man is going to do next.

Thousands of repetitions are needed to get the throws accurate. Ultimately, the aim is to do them without having to think about them, as a kind of conditioned reflex. We are all familiar with the situation where we do something quite casually, such as throwing our hat onto a hat peg, and when it comes off, we say, 'I couldn't do that again, if I tried', and we couldn't. True judo is rather like that. It happens, rather than being consciously done. But behind this 'happening', with its deceptive ease, lie the years of practice.

CHAPTER FOUR
Groundwork : Holdings

It is generally considered in judo circles that an assailant who was thrown heavily with one of the throws already described, would be unable to continue to fight if he landed on a hard surface without knowing how to fall. This is probably true, as he would be most likely to hit his head if he did not know the breakfalls described in the previous chapter.

In case further measures should be necessary, however, judo students learn various groundwork movements. In this chapter, and the next two, we shall examine the commoner ones.

What are called 'holdings', or osae komi waza, are learnt first. These are methods of controlling the opponent without actually hurting him, so that he cannot get away. They would, for example, enable one to hold a ruffian until the police arrived.

They are learnt first because until you can control the movements of your opponent the armlocks and strangleholds of the next two chapters are useless. He would be able to move out of them.

In judo contest, groundwork can be done if one man is thrown, but not sufficiently cleanly to gain a point. Alternatively, if the contestants do not wish to do groundwork, they can stand up again and continue the fight on their feet.

The important thing to remember about holdings is to relax, sagging as much of your weight as possible onto the opponent, like a dead weight. If you stiffen up you will find that you are taking some of the weight off him and the hold is then less effective.

To gain a point in a judo contest you have to hold the opponent for thirty seconds after the referee has indicated that he recognises the hold. It is considered that if the opponent cannot get out in thirty seconds, he never will. At any time, either in a holding or under an armlock or stranglehold, the opponent may submit. To do so he lightly taps either the opponent or the mat with a hand or foot. He must be instantly released on giving this signal of submission. Alternatively, he might say that he gives in.

We shall study eleven holdings.

1. *Scarf Hold* (Kesa Gatame)

Your partner is lying flat on his back. Sit at his right side. With your left hand, hold his jacket at his right shoulder and trap his right arm under your left armpit. Your stomach should be close up under his right armpit. Bend your right knee and take it forwards under his right arm. Take your left leg out at right angles to his body, bending it at the knee if desired. Put your right arm under his head from his left side, with the palm of the hand on the ground. From this position, put your right hip bone in his solar plexus and slide your body to his right. Relax all your weight on him, keeping your head forwards and to the left of his head (as viewed by you), i.e., over his right shoulder. See Figure 94.

Hold tight and if he moves around in his efforts to dislodge you move with him, maintaining the same relative positions of your bodies and legs. Do not let him trap your left leg by bringing his right foot over it. He will probably try to sit up. Counter this by moving your left foot back. He will vary this with trying to buck you over his head, placing his feet on the floor and lifting his hips to do so. Counter this by crossing your left leg over your right and pushing yourself back down. He may try to grasp you around the waist and roll you over his body to his left. Stretch out your right arm and put the hand on the floor to push yourself back.

Relax entirely. If you stiffen up you are like a board. He has only to lift part of your weight, since the other is taken on that part of you that remains on the floor. If you relax you are like a sack of sand. As he lifts one part of you, the weight runs to another and his efforts are frustrated.

He is not allowed to hit or press nerve centres, nor to push the face, but he can put his hand under your chin to push your head back. He would try this with his free hand, of course, so tuck your chin in, keeping your head down and close to the right side of his head.

If he succeeds in freeing his right arm from your left armpit, the hold is considered broken and the count would stop in a judo contest. The referee would then order you both to resume your feet, unless you moved into another hold or continued to struggle for an armlock or stranglehold, or he was attempting counterholds against you.

2. *Shoulder Hold* (Kata Gatame)

This is done from the same position as the last hold but the opponent does free his right arm by pulling it out. As he does so, push on his right elbow so as to take it across his throat. With your left hand, catch your right, turning the arm so that the bone on the thumb edge of the arm is against the back of his neck. Pull your right arm up with your left hand and put your head on the ground, tight against his right upper arm so as to press it to the side of his head. Hold tight and move around with him as before. See Figure 95.

This hold sometimes partly strangles the opponent, in which case he will give in by tapping. Be prepared to let him go immediately he does so.

You may vary the position of your feet in this hold by coming up onto your right knee, keeping it close to his side, and stretching your left leg back with the toes in the mat. Then, use this outstretched left leg to push your own head into the mat above his right shoulder.

The opponent may try to turn onto his face, or to do a back somersault, or to loosen your grip by pushing his right arm against the side of your head with his left. Be prepared for any of these manoeuvres. Hold tight and try to main-

94

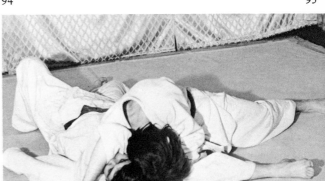

95

96

97

tain the same relative positions.

3. *Side Four Quarters* (Yoko Shiho Gatame)

Kneel at the opponent's right side, facing him. With your left hand catch his left shoulder, holding the jacket, of course, and passing your left arm under his head to do so. Pull the shoulder to the ground by means of the jacket. Pass your right arm between his legs and catch either his belt or the tail of his jacket if you cannot reach his belt. Lower your weight forwards so that you are lying across his body with your head on the left-hand side. Relax all your weight on his body. Stretch your legs out behind you, spread them wide apart and dig your toes into the mat. Lower your stomach. Take as little weight as possible on your own toes or elbows. Put as much as you can on the partner. See Figure 96.

If he moves around, move around with him, maintaining the same relative positions. He may try to roll to his left. If he does, put your head on the ground to push yourself back. He may put his feet on the ground and bridge with the object of turning quickly towards you. Sag your weight on to him and with both hands pull in the direction of your own knees. He may try with his left forearm to push the side of your neck and take your head far enough down his body to bring his left leg over your head. This is a bad position for you and may lead to an armlock on your left arm. To avoid it, as soon as you see his intention keep your head well up towards his left shoulder so that he cannot get his forearm against your neck. If he does, instantly put your head on the ground close to his left thigh so that he cannot get his leg over your head. If he has got it over, let go with your left hand and bring the arm into your body out of danger. But remember that, in doing this, you will have lost the hold and must move into another. Moving into the next hold (no. 4) is a possible move from this situation.

4. *Upper Four Quarters* (Kami Shiho Gatame)

The opponent is lying along a line. Kneel behind his head, facing him and on the same line. Pass both hands under his shoulders and catch his belt at either side of his body. Pull it to the ground so that the piece of his belt on top of him and between your hands is holding him down. Lower your body forwards so that your stomach is on his face and your chin in his stomach, or as near these positions as is possible, bearing in mind your relative heights. Spread your legs wide apart and dig your toes into the mat. Lower your stomach and relax all your weight onto him. This hold partially smothers an opponent so, for practice, allow him to turn his head to one side so that he may continue to breathe. See Figure 97.

Maintain the same relative position, moving with him if he moves. There must be a straight line through his body and your's. If he can disturb this straight line he may be able to sit up, or do a backwards somersault. The usual way to try and escape, however, is to try and turn you over, by bridging, grasping your belt with both hands and then dropping one leg through the gap made by the bridge. If it succeeds, he has exactly the same hold on you. The answer is to pull down strongly on the side he is trying to raise with the hand and to extend the opposite foot still wider to prevent the turn. It is a question of leverage. If he is trying to lift his right hip, then the force he can exert is equal to 'effort times effort arm', according to the laws of mechanics. The 'effort arm' in this case is half the distance between his hips. Your resisting force is equal to 'resistance times resistance arm'. The 'resistance arm' will be the distance between your outstretched left foot and the extension of the line drawn centrally up his body. Thus the wider your foot is placed, the greater the resistance arm. Suppose half the distance between his hips to be 6in, and the distance your foot is out from the central line to be 24in. Let x equal the force he is using to try to raise his hip, and y the power you are using to stop him. Then 6x equals 24y.

$$\text{Or } \frac{x}{y} = \frac{24}{6}$$

The effort he will have to exert is therefore four times the resistance you can call upon, and your resistance potential is your total weight, if you relax. Plainly, then, you must have him at a disadvantage.

The scientific explanation of one's power in relation to this holding has been given as an example but anyone interested in this aspect of judo can work out for himself the mechanical advantage in most of the movements, both throwing and on the ground. It is interesting to do so, since it explains why often a frail girl or a young boy can overcome a mature man of less skill or knowledge.

5. *Broken Upper Four Quarters* (Kuzure Kami Shiho Gatame)

This is a hold from behind, as in the last case. Kneel behind the opponent's head. Keep the same straight line through your bodies. With your left arm passing under his left shoulder, seize his belt at his left side and pull down, as in the last hold. But pass your right arm over his and take the hand up to seize his collar at the back of his neck. Trap his right arm to your right side with your elbow. Now spread your legs as before, lower your body, and put your chin in his stomach. Your right leg in this hold is, however, rather over to your right and your stomach tends to be on his right shoulder, holding that down, rather than on his face. Relax completely. See Figure 98.

In all these holds it helps to watch the opponent's breathing and to flop all your weight on him as he breathes out, making it that much more difficult for him to breathe in again. The methods by which he will attempt to get out of this hold are exactly the same as for the last hold. Simply relax, maintain the same relative positions, move with him, spread your legs as needed to stop him turning you and keep his right arm trapped to your right side.

6. *Rear Scarf Hold* (Gyaku Kesa Gatame)

Take up the position described in the last hold, so that you begin by actually doing the last hold. Now come up on your knees and take your left leg through and under your right, and apply your left hip to the side of his head. Your left leg is now bent and stretches out at roughly right angles to his body; your right leg stretches out behind you. Relax your weight on his head and hold tight with your hands. See Figure 99.

This is an extremely difficult hold to get out of and the weight on the opponent's head often produces a submission. Do not let him get his head or his arm out, and maintain the same relative positions by moving with him and changing direction with him.

7. *Chest Locking* (Mune Gatame)

Kneel facing him at his right side. Lean across his body. With your right hand catch his jacket

98

99

100

101

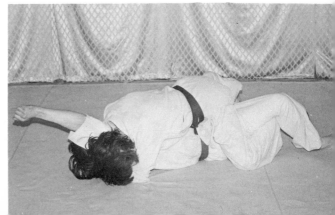

at about shoulder level on his left sleeve. Put your right elbow against his left hip. With your left arm passing over his body, not under his head, rest your elbow on the ground near his left shoulder and catch his belt with the left hand. Keep your right knee against his right hip and stretch out your left leg at right angles to his body, digging your toes into the mat. Keep his hips pressed tight between your right knee and your right elbow, so that he cannot turn either way. Relax your weight on him. See Figure 100.

This is a very strong hold. His only real hope is to turn over, so he will try to widen the gap between your right knee and your right elbow to give him the necessary space. Do not let him. He may try to catch your left foot in his right hand so as to lift you, combining this with a turn. He may try to sit up, alternating this with trying to buck you up his body. Just relax, hold tight and move around with him to maintain the same relative positions.

8. *Lengthways Four Quarters* (Tate Shiho Gatame)

The partner is lying flat on his back with his feet on the ground and knees raised. Kneel astride him and tuck your feet around his legs from the outside, so that your feet catch the insides of his calves. Get his right arm above his head and fold your own arms around his arm and head, your forearms being under his head. It is the same action as 'folding one's arms' in school. Your folded arms trap his right arm to the right side of his head. Take your own head forwards to the ground above his right shoulder and relax. You can spread his legs slightly, but this may hurt him and, if it does, it would be counted as a leg lock and banned in judo contests. So be careful about this. See Figure 101.

He will try to free a leg, Simply catch it again. He will try to turn you over. Simply spread the leg in the direction he is trying to take you. Sag all your weight on to him.

9. *Broken Scarf Hold* (Kuzure Kesa Gatame)

Take up first the position of the Scarf Hold (no. 1 in this chapter). Now sit up and trap his left arm under your right, in the same way as you are trapping his right arm under your left. Hold with both hands at the respective shoulders, your left holding his right and your right his

left. Take your right bent leg farther forwards beyond his right shoulder. Now you must put your right hip bone on him and rest your weight on it, choosing the exact position where he can neither sit up nor buck you over his head. With both hands and arms, keep his shoulders off the ground. See Figure 102.

His only way out is either to buck you over his head, holding your belt with both hands to assist this move, or to sit up and take you backwards. To buck you, he has first got to get his shoulders on the ground. Stop him. To sit up, he has got to shift your weight down his body. Keep it at the exact spot.

10. *Head Locking* (Kashira Gatame)

This is much the same as the Scarf Hold (no. 1 in this chapter) but with one difference. Your right hand, instead of resting on the ground, catches your own right trouser leg at the inside of the knee. It makes the hold that much stronger. See Figure 103.

The methods of attempted escape and their counters are all as described in no. 1 of this chapter.

11. *Broken Side Four Quarters* (Kuzure Yoko Shiho Gatame)

This, again, is almost exactly the same as the side four quarters (no. 3 in this chapter), but your left hand, instead of passing behind his head, passes over his throat and holds the shoulder to the ground as before. See Figure 104.

A permissible variation with the right hand is not to put it between his legs, but to pass it under his body and catch his left sleeve at the edge, so holding his left arm to his side. Relax on him as before. The methods of attempted escape are all the same.

With this particular hold, of course, you can move on to the strangulation of the partner simply by bringing your left elbow to the ground so that the bony outer edge of your left arm presses against the front of his throat. Bear all your weight on it and he will give in.

The secrets of success in all these holdings are to keep your body as low as possible, to relax, and to put as much weight as possible on the opponent, supporting as little as possible on your own arms or legs. Even when you fail to hold him for the full thirty seconds in a judo contest, the struggle to escape often exhausts him so much that he is unequal to continuing the struggle when you resume a standing position. From these holding positions you can move to armlocks and strangles as described in the chapters which follow. You can also change from one holding position to another. If you do so without losing control of your opponent, the count would still go on in judo contest.

There is room for much experimentation and improvising in groundwork. The only way to become a master at it is to practise with a keen partner and to work out moves for yourself. It is a cross between wrestling and chess, where you are trying to see several moves ahead and to trap your opponent into making a false move. Almost every muscle of the body is brought into play in groundwork, and the exercise is comparable to Yoga in the benefits it confers.

102

103

104

CHAPTER FIVE
Groundwork : Armlocks

There are only two basic armlocks: the straight armlock, in which pressure is put on the elbow joint and the arm bent back against it, causing pain or dislocation; and the bent armlock, in which an attempt is made to turn the arm out of the shoulder socket. All known armlocks are a variation on either of these, though there are dozens of them, all under different names. We shall be looking at five in this chapter, but bear in mind that whenever an arm is straight, if you can put part of your body or limb behind the elbow and bend the arm back against it, you will be doing a straight armlock in essence.

In practising these armlocks it is vital that you should realise how dangerous they can be. You can get into the position of applying them as quickly as you like, but you must not apply them with a jerk, or violently. Pressure must be put on carefully, and you must be prepared to stop the instant your opponent signals his surrender. As previously mentioned, he does this either by tapping or by saying that he gives in.

1. Cross Armlock (Juji Gatame)

Sit at the right side of your partner about the level of his shoulder. Put your left leg across his throat with the foot on the ground to stop him sitting up. Put your right toes under his right side, knee bent. Hold his right arm at the wrist with both your hands, keeping it between your legs. Lie back and put your head on the ground. Keep your knees together. Now note on which side of his arm is his little finger. You will find that his elbow is on the same side. If it is to your right, take the elbow joint back against your right inside thigh and gently press back on the wrist until he gives in. See Figure 105.

If his little finger is to your left, take the elbow against the inside of your left thigh and press back on the wrist until he submits. If the elbow is directly underneath, hold his wrist to your chest and raise your stomach so that it is pressing upon his elbow joint. Either of these moves will produce instant submission.

2. Entangled Armlock (Ude Garami)

Lie across your partner from his right side to his left, so that your weight is holding his chest down. Bend his left arm upwards at the elbow joint so that the upper arm is at right angles to his body and the forearm is bent back towards his head at an angle of approximately 45 degrees to the upper arm. Put your left hand on his wrist, fingers uppermost and keep your forearm level and low down. Pass your right arm under the upper part of his left and rest the hand on your own left wrist, fingers uppermost. Keep your elbow down and your arm level with the ground. See Figure 106.

Now simply turn both your wrists gently down towards the ground. The effect is to twist his arm at the shoulder socket and he will submit.

3. Arm Crush (Ude Gatame)

This is one of the variations of the straight armlock. Kneel at the opponent's right side with your left knee on the ground and your right knee raised, toes under him. The lock is applied when, from this position, he raises his left arm to grasp your lapel. Clasp both your hands over his elbow joint, turning it away from your own body. Turn his body onto his right side and kneel on it with your right knee to hold him there. Press down on his wrist and hand with your shoulder, and pull the elbow in towards your chest. See Figure 107.

The moral of this armlock is never to reach up a straight arm to catch hold of an opponent

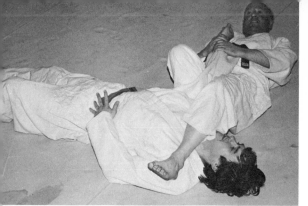

05   106

109

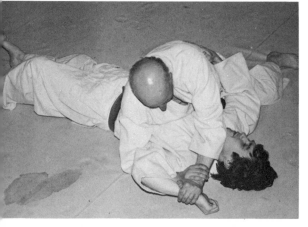

07   108

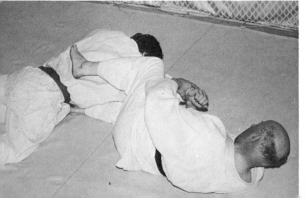

if he is in a position to control your body.

4. *Knee Armlock* (Hiza Gatame)

This again is a straight armlock. Your partner is between your legs and incautiously reaches out a hand to grasp your collar as a preliminary, perhaps, to strangling you. Suppose it is his right arm. Catch his wrist with both your hands and pull to keep the arm straight. If he is on his knees, push his left knee away with your right foot and roll to your right, so that you are on your right side. Raise your left leg and bend it at the knee. Place the knee on the back of his elbow. Turn his wrist so that his little finger edge is uppermost, so making sure that his elbow joint is in contact with your knee. Now lift gently with your hands. See Figure 108.

5. *Leg Armlock* (Ashi Gatame)

Proceed exactly as for the previous armlock, but instead of putting your knee against the back of his elbow take your foot over his arm and put it under his chin. Now, if you straighten your leg and pull with your hands to keep his arm straight, you will have the leg armlock. See Figure 109.

Both these armlocks illustrate the principle that to get between your opponent's legs is to put yourself in a weak position. On no account reach out your arms to strangle him from this position or you will be open to one of these armlocks. Get out from between his legs before you do anything else.

If, of course, your partner reaches out both hands and not just one, which is what would normally happen, you can still apply these two locks by concentrating on one arm only. Whichever arm you choose to apply the lock on, roll the opposite way.

55

CHAPTER SIX
Groundwork : Strangleholds

Some judo strangleholds have as their object constriction of the windpipe to restrict breathing, while the purpose of others is to constrict the carotid arteries and by so restricting the flow of blood to the brain to cause loss of consciousness. We shall make it clear which are which in the course of the descriptions. As with the armlocks, remember that these are extremely dangerous and must be practised with great care, and never applied with a jerk. If they are applied seriously, loss of consciousness can ensue in from anything from two to eight seconds, depending upon the opponent's experience of resisting them. So be prepared to let him go the instant he gives in, which he will have to signify by tapping since one cannot normally speak in these locks. If he loses consciousness, let him go at once. If you continue to hold after he has lost consciousness, he will be dead in about five seconds.

As with armlocks, successful application of strangleholds depends upon your ability to control the movement of your opponent's body, otherwise he may be able to twist out of them. So, for those where you are on top, remember to keep your full weight on him.

We are going to look at nine movements. Most of them could be applied even if you were in the underneath position on the ground, so it is not necessarily the worst position to be in. All of them could be applied against a standing opponent but their use in this way, though not forbidden, is not encouraged in judo contests. Submission in a judo contest would lose a point, of course, and the other man would win, but do not hesitate to submit if you are caught. It is better to lose than be killed.

1. *Normal Cross* (Nami Juji Jime)
Kneel astride the partner, controlling him with your knees pressed to his sides. Cross your arms normally, that is with the palms down. Put the thumbs inside his collar: the right thumb inside his right collar, the left thumb inside his left collar. Put them as far back as possible. Pull with both hands towards your own body, parting the elbows. See Figure 110.

This is one of the strangleholds that restricts the flow of blood to the brain. The bony edges of your arms dig into the sides of his neck. Do not turn your wrists to the position where the fleshy part behind or in front of your arms is against his throat, as this will be less effective. If you do not get almost instantaneous submission from this necklock, you are probably not applying it correctly. Practise it more.

2. *Reverse Cross* (Gyaku Juji Jime)
This is the same as for the previous stranglehold except that, when you cross your arms, you do so with the palms upwards and so insert your fingers inside his collar, thumbs outside. See Figure 111.

Again, it restricts the flow of blood to the brain.

3. *Half Cross* (Kata Juji Jime)
This is a hold that constricts the windpipe. Kneel astride your partner, keeping your knees at his side to control him and sitting on his stomach. Put your right thumb inside his right collar just behind his right ear. Turn your right arm so that the bony edge on the little finger side rests across the front of his throat, and lower your elbow so that the arm is parallel to the ground. With your left hand, catch his left lapel just below the collar bone, fingers inside thumb outside. See Figure 112.

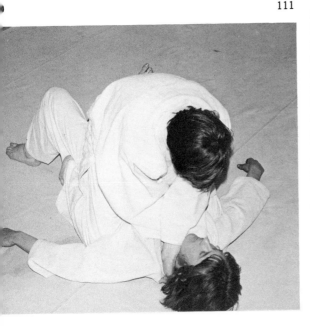

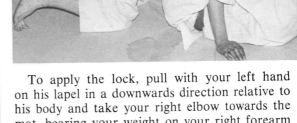

To apply the lock, pull with your left hand on his lapel in a downwards direction relative to his body and take your right elbow towards the mat, bearing your weight on your right forearm which is across his throat. It is a painful lock, so be careful. Submission will be rapid.

4. *Lateral Cross* (Yoko Juji Jime)

Take up the position of the reverse cross (no. 2 in this chapter). To relieve the pressure upon him, the opponent may try to push your elbows together. If he does, roll onto your right side and right over onto your back, maintaining the stranglehold and bringing him with you. He will now be on top of you and between your legs. Bend your knees and put your two feet in his sides, just under his hip bones. Lift him off the ground with your feet whilst continuing to apply the stranglehold. He is now in such a weak position that he cannot resist. See Figure 113.

5. *Sliding Collar* (Okuri Eri)

This stranglehold and the four which follow are applied from behind the partner. To practise them, let him sit up while you kneel on your left knee directly behind him, with your right foot up. In reality, of course, they could be applied on the ground, whenever he turned his back to you or from a standing position if you were behind the opponent. They are particularly used against an opponent who is so incautious as to get up with his back to you. Always, when rising from the ground, you should face your opponent and be ready to defend yourself.

From the practice position of kneeling behind the partner, put your right arm round his neck from the rear, that is over his right shoulder and across the front of his neck. With the right hand, grasp his left collar, thumb inside and fingers out, well back behind his left ear. Pass your left arm under his left armpit and catch his right lapel at the level of his upper chest. Pull down with your left hand towards the floor and back with your right forearm, taking your right elbow back. Be sure to bring him off balance to his rear. See Figure 114.

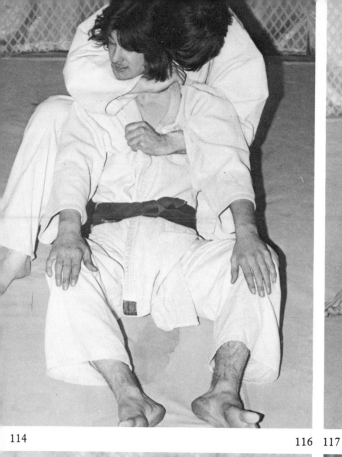

114

1

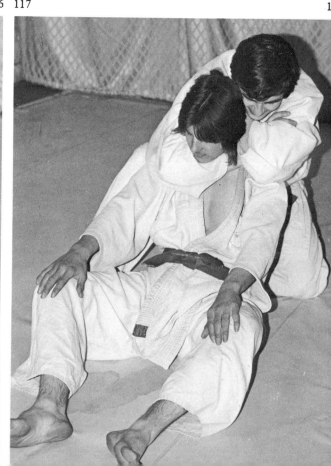

8   The right wrist digs into the carotid artery on his left and the tightened jacket prevents him moving his head away from this pressure. It restricts the flow of blood to the brain.

6. Single Wing Necklock (Kata Ha Jime)

This is similar to the last one. The right arm passes over the opponent's right shoulder, across the front of his throat, while the right hand catches his left collar just behind his left ear, thumb inside and fingers out as before. But the left arm, having passed under his left armpit, comes up over his left shoulder and across the back of his neck. Some referees will not allow you to use the left hand to push his head forwards, but the same effect is achieved by sliding the left forearm across the back of his neck, as though sawing. Pull him off balance backwards. See Figure 115.

The neck is caught between the bony thumb-side edge of the right arm in front and the bony little finger-side edge of the left forearm behind. It constricts the windpipe and may also have effect on the left carotid artery as well.

7. Naked Necklock (Ushiro Jime)

This one is so called because it could be applied to an opponent who was not wearing a jacket. From the practice position on one knee behind him, pass your right arm over your partner's right shoulder, with the forearm across the front of his throat and the bony edge of the thumb side in contact with his throat. Pass your left hand over his left shoulder and, with fingers uppermost and thumb underneath, catch your own right wrist. The back of your right hand is uppermost. Pull back on your right wrist with your left hand to exert pressure against the front of his throat. At the same time, put your right shoulder behind his head and push it forwards to prevent him relieving the pressure by bringing his head back. See Figure 116.

This constricts the windpipe and is painful.

8. Necklock from Rear (Hadaka Jime)

Sometimes called the 'Japanese stranglehold', this also could be applied against an opponent who was not wearing a jacket. From the kneeling position behind the partner, pass your right arm over his right shoulder and imprison his neck in the 'V' of your elbow joint by bending your arm. Bend your left arm and put your right hand in the 'V' of your left elbow, fingers uppermost. Put your left hand on the back of his head. See Figure 117.

The muscle of your right upper arm presses against his right carotid artery, the bony edge of the thumb side of your forearm presses against his left carotid artery, and your left hand prevents him moving his head back to relieve these pressures. The effect is to restrict the flow of blood to the brain.

9. Sleeve Wheel (Sode Guruma)

From the kneeling position behind the opponent, pass your left arm over his right shoulder and catch his left lapel, thumb inside, fingers outside. Pass your right arm over the top of your left and over his left shoulder, and catch the same lapel (his left) about two inches above your left hand hold, again with thumb inside and fingers out. Pull back with both hands so that the bit of his lapel between your hands presses against the front of his throat. See Figure 118.

This has a double effect. The jacket against your opponent's windpipe restricts his breathing, while the bony edges of your forearms against the sides of his neck restrict the flow of blood to his brain.

CHAPTER SEVEN
Nage No Kata

Nage No Kata is a formal demonstration of judo throws. Before proceeding to a detailed study of it, a few words should be said about katas in general.

Katas are an attempt to preserve in their purest forms the knowledge of techniques. One man acts as the performer of the techniques. He is called Tori. The other has the techniques applied to him. He is called Uke. Uke gives Tori the perfect opportunity to apply the technique, and Tori's application must be absolutely accurate as regards timing, form, and complete control of his partner. They work together in harmony, striving between them to give a perfect demonstration of movements done under the most favourable circumstances. Thus, by this ritual performance, they preserve the knowledge of the purest form of the technique and the precise moment at which to apply it.

Kata is both the art and the science of judo. It has also been called the grammar of judo, and a study of it can do much to improve one's contest ability, as it gives practice in perfect timing and co-ordination of movements. To encourage such a study, kata competitions are sometimes held in conjunction with judo championships.

One or more katas are usually performed on ceremonial occasions, such as the re-opening of the dojo after holidays, or at gradings, public displays, or in honour of a distinguished visitor to the dojo. They are usually performed by the highest grades, as long practice with the partner is essential before they can be attempted in public. Nage No Kata and Katame No Kata (dealt with in the next chapter) are part of the required test for the black belt.

The sequence of movements that comprise the kata is a complete entity. Everything must be accurate, from the first bow to the distinguished guests to the last bow. Every single movement, every gesture, has its meaning and purpose. There must be no unnecessary movements nor anything that is not part of the kata. Between movements partners must remain absolutely still.

Study of the throws and their precise moment of execution will be of special interest to those attracted by the scientific aspects of judo, since they can work out how maximum effect is obtained with minimum effort. Similarly, those to whom judo has an aesthetic appeal will find in the controlled perfection of movements in kata an art form akin to ballet.

Katas must be performed honestly. The throws are generally made in response to an attacking movement by the partner, and that attack must be genuine. Even in Kime No Kata, where some of the attacks are made with dagger or sword, it would be considered a disgrace to give a dishonest or faked performance of the kata.

Although katas were devised as a ritual to preserve the ancient forms for all time, over the years variations have crept in. One master will teach one form, another a different one, but always the same basic sequence will be followed. To try and rationalise this situation, the Japanese masters held a conference in the 1960s to try and agree on a standard form of the various katas. Not all the masters accept the version produced by that conference, so all that any book can do is to set out the basic form. If your particular teacher prefers a slightly different variation, listen to him. He may well be just as right as another teacher who has studied under a different master.

It should be emphasised, however, that these variations are minor. The basic sequence and the basic approach are not in dispute. Such variations, indeed, are almost inevitable since any art is subjective and one could well liken them to the different readings of an orchestral score by various conductors. The student can only listen to all the masters he meets and eventually produce his own rendering.

Nage No Kata, which was created by Professor Jigoro Kano, who based it on his study of the ancient techniques, consists of five sets of throws, three in each set. The first set consists of hand throws (Te Waza), the second of hip throws (Koshi Waza), the third of foot throws (Ashi Waza), the fourth of sacrifice throws in which the thrower falls on his back (Masutemi Waza), while the last set comprises sacrifice throws in which the thrower falls on his side (Yoko Sutemi Waza).

The honoured guests at the demonstration will be seated together at one side of the mat, their seat being known as the 'joseki'. As the performance is in their honour, it must be directed towards them and even in practice the performers will bow to the joseki and not turn their backs to it unnecessarily.

Tori (the thrower) will stand to the left of the joseki, as viewed by anyone seated in the high seat, and Uke (the one who is thrown) will stand to the right. They will stand for a few seconds absolutely upright and still, approximately twelve feet apart. Then, simultaneously, they will turn approximately thirty degrees so that they each face the joseki and bow to it. Heels must be together, hands at sides, and costumes impeccably arranged. See Figure 119.

They will then turn back to face each other and bow. Both bows are normally made from the standing position. See Figure 120.

Each then steps forwards one pace, left foot first, then right, bringing their feet to the normal distance apart, since they have been standing heels together for the bow. See Figure 121.

From this point on, visualise a line drawn between them. This is the axis of the kata. All throws are done down this axis, first on the normal side, then with the partners at opposite ends on the opposite side, so that there are two repetitions of each throw. Many throws involve three steps being taken, each unbalancing Uke a little more, with the throw on the third step.

119

120

121

All this will become clear as we proceed to the details of throws. You are Tori, the thrower; your partner is Uke, the man who is thrown.

SET ONE (HAND THROWS)

1. *Uki Otoshi*

Walk normally towards your partner, straight up the axis of the kata, until you are the right distance from him for both of you to reach out and take the normal holds. You must be upright, looking him straight in the face, and making no unnecessary movements, such as swinging the arms. He must be perfectly still and relaxed. When you are at the correct distance, pause a moment.

Then, as you simultaneously take the normal holds on each other, step back with your left foot and bring your right nearly up to it, in the Tsugi Ashi movement described in Chapter 1. Uke follows your movements by advancing with his right foot and bringing his left nearly up to it, also with the Tsugi Ashi movement, so that as you break his balance forwards with your steps backwards, he recovers with his steps forwards. See Figure 122.

Repeat this move exactly, but this time stepping a little farther back and breaking your partner's balance a little more markedly. He recovers by following your foot moves, as before.

Now repeat the move a third time, but on this occasion step back a pace and a half with your left foot and drop onto your left knee. Your partner, being unable to recover from this unbalancing, will somersault forwards if you pull with both hands down towards your own left belt. Note that when you kneel on your left knee, your toes are in the mat. This is always so when you are throwing and the instep is off the mat, unlike when you are doing the kneeling salutation. See Figure 123 for the throw.

This form of Uki Ostoshi varies from that described in Set Four, no. 8 of The Gokyo, in that the thrower is kneeling to perform it, but in essence it is the same throw.

Your partner has landed behind you. He will rise and go to your end of the kata. Get up and follow him until you reach the distance where you can take the usual holds. This time, take exactly the opposite holds; that is, catch hold of his left sleeve with your right hand and his right

lapel with your left hand. When you step back to perform the throw your first step is with your right foot, he following with his left. Simply reverse all the directions for the normal performance of the throw and you will have the way to do it on his left side.

It is important that whenever you or your partner turn round at the end of the kata axis, or indeed anywhere else, you should turn towards the joseki and not away from it.

2. *Seoi Nage*

The preceding movements have left you at your right end of the kata axis, since the second performance of Uki Otoshi took your partner to his own end.

You now advance with normal steps to a distance of six feet from your partner. You are going to do the shoulder throw in response to an attack by him.

He steps forwards with his left foot and takes his right arm back behind him, ready to swing up and over and to strike you on top of the skull with the base of his clenched fist. This blow is one of the 'atemi', or blows at vital spots practised under the old ju-jitsu systems. It is the bottom strike first (tettsui) of karate.

As he is advancing his left foot you must bear in mind that, when he strikes, he will try to bring his right foot forwards and past his left. His moment of greatest weakness from the judo point of view will be when his feet are in line, as at that moment his balance can be broken directly forwards. So, timing your movement to correspond exactly with his, when you see his left foot advancing, advance your right diagonally forwards and place it just inside the position where his right is going to come. At the same time raise both your arms so that the blow, when it comes, will pass between them. See Figure 124.

Your partner now strikes the blow, bringing his right foot forwards as he does so, but the blow passes over your right shoulder as you turn and take your left foot back and around to a position just inside his left. You then seize his sleeve and jacket at the shoulder with left and right hands respectively, and you are in a position to do the shoulder throw, Seoi Nage, described in Set One, no. 8, of The Gokyo. See Figure 125.

You perform the throw, taking care to sup-

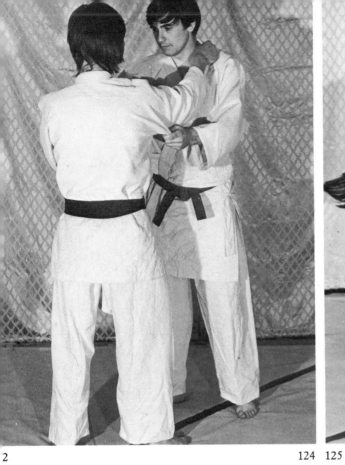

port your partner as he falls. He gets up and goes to your end of the kata axis. You follow to a distance of six feet and the throw is repeated on the left-hand side, as before, thus taking you both to your own ends of the kata axis.

It should be noted that all throws must be executed directly along the line of the kata. The partner must not be thrown off at a tangent.

3. *Kata Guruma*

For the third throw, you come to the distance where you can take the normal holds. You catch simultaneously and as you retreat he advances, in exactly the same movements as for the first throw (Uki Otoshi). The first step is exactly the same.

You repeat this step a second time, but as you are doing so you must change your left hand hold on his right sleeve. Let go and, passing your hand under his arm, catch his sleeve on the inside with your palm towards his arm, fingers up and thumb down. See Figure 126.

Now when you step back the third time with your left foot, you leave the right behind and pull your partner's arm up and forwards over the back of your neck, as you insert your right shoulder under his right hip. Let go with your right hand and catch his right trousers just behind the knee from the inside, so that you are in the position to perform Kata Guruma as described in Set Three, no. 8, of The Gokyo. See Figure 127.

Lift the partner onto your shoulders. See Figure 128.

Turn to face down the line of the kata to your own end as you throw, and support the partner strongly with a pull up on his right sleeve. See Figure 129.

Go to the other end of the kata axis and repeat the throw on the left-hand side, and this will bring you both back to your own ends.

To mark this ending of the first set of throws, there is now a slight pause. Standing at your own ends of the kata, you turn your backs on each other, but not on the joseki, and adjust your judo suits. In theory, this is done simply by grasping the bottom front corner of the jacket, one flap in one hand and one in the other, and pulling it straight. In practice, however, rather more re-arrangement of one's attire is necessary, but it should be done with as little fuss as possible.

When you are both ready, you turn simultaneously to face each other for the second set. Ideally, you should know each other's movements and be able to time things so well that you make a simultaneous turn without any signal passing between you.

SET TWO (HIP THROWS)

1. *Uki Goshi*

As for the shoulder throw (the second one in the last group), this throw is made in response to an attempt by your partner to strike you on top of the head with the bottom of his right fist.

You advance to a distance of about six feet from him, whereupon he advances his left foot and take his right arm back to strike. Again, his position of greatest weakness is going to be when his feet are in line, but this time you are going to throw on his left-hand side.

As he advances his left foot you must advance your left, stepping diagonally forwards and placing it just inside his left, and turning on it. You must time this so that your actions are simultaneous. Then, as he advances his right, you take your right back and round in a small circle, and place it just inside where his right is going to be. His blow passes over your right shoulder. Your left arm goes round his waist at the back and your right hand catches the sleeve of his left arm which he has held slightly forwards for that purpose. See Figure 130.

You are now in a position to do Uki Goshi, the floating loin throw, described in Set One, no. 4, of The Gokyo, though remember that you are doing it on his left-hand side, not on his right as described in The Gokyo.

When he has been thrown, he gets up and goes to your end of the kata axis. You follow and stand at a distance of six feet, ready for the repetition on the other side which will bring you back to your own ends.

2. *Harai Goshi*

This throw is one of those performed from the three-step movement, like the first throw in the first set (Uki Otoshi). Your first movements therefore are exactly the same. You advance to distance for taking normal holds, take hold and move, so breaking his balance forwards.

Now, on the second repeat, you change your

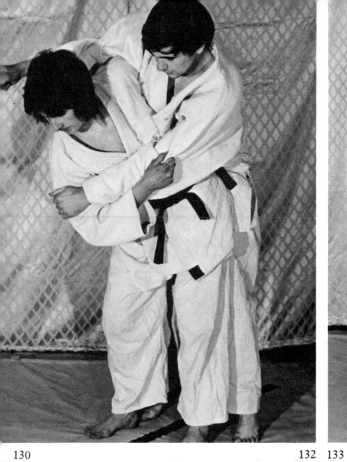

right hand hold by letting go of his left lapel and passing your right arm under his left armpit and behind his back, resting the flat of the hand on his right shoulder blade. See Figure 131.

Your third step is as follows. Take your left foot back very quickly and around behind you in a small circle, and place it just inside his left foot. Turn your back on him at the same time. Now, as he advances his right foot, your right sweeps it away and you throw him with the sweeping hip throw (Harai Goshi) as described in Set Two, no. 7, of The Gokyo. See Figure 132.

You will see that the third step with your left foot back and around has to be made very quickly indeed, since you have to do it and sweep with your right in the time that your partner is advancing his right. You must catch him in his advance.

Again the throw is repeated on the other side, taking you to your own ends of the kata.

3. Tsurikomi Goshi

This is another of the three-step moves. Advance and take the normal holds. Take the first step as in Uki Otoshi. On the second step, you change your right hand hold by taking it further up his left lapel and onto his left collar. See Figure 133.

On the third step, you take your left foot back and round in a small circle, turning your back on your partner and bringing your right foot to just inside his right, so that you are in a position to perform O Goshi on him (Set One, no. 6, of The Gokyo). See Figure 134.

He must be clearly seen to resist this attempt by straightening up and thrusting his stomach forwards. To counter this, you bend your knees much more so that your hips are in contact with his front thighs and you are able to perform the resisting hip throw (Tsurikomi Goshi) as described in Set Two, no. 4, of The Gokyo. See Figure 135.

As usual, the throw is repeated on the opposite side from the other end of the kata axis, bringing you back to your own ends.

This marks the end of the second set, so again there is a pause during which you simultaneously turn your backs to each other, adjust your jackets, and then turn to face each other again.

SET THREE (FOOT THROWS)

1. Okuri Ashi Barai

You both advance to the centre of the kata and as you take the normal holds you both turn to a position on either side of the axis. You turn by stepping forwards with your left foot and bringing your right into line. Your partner, who has done the same, now has his back to the joseki, while you are facing it. As you turn, you take the normal holds on each other. See Figure 136.

Now, moving in unison, you both take three rapid steps, you to your right, he to his left. He begins with his left foot and you move your right in time with it. He brings his right foot up to it and, as he does so, you slightly unbalance him to his right side by lifting with your right hand on his lapel and pulling down slightly with your left on his sleeve. On the first two of these steps, you simply move your left foot up in time with his right, but on the third step you use this left to sweep his right into his left, strengthening the lift with your right hand and the pull-down with your right so that you throw him with Okuri Ashi Barai (the double ankle sweep) described in Set Two, no. 5, of The Gokyo. See Figure 137.

You are really floating him onto his toes in the first two steps, and sweeping on the third. When he falls, he gets up in exactly that spot. You take the opposite holds and this time he moves to his right and you to your left, so that you repeat the throw on the other side.

2. Sasae Tsurikomi Ashi

This again is one of the three-step throws, like Uki Otoshi.

Come in to normal holds distance. Catch and move exactly as for the first throw in the first set. Unbalance your partner as you move with a slight lift-pull action of your left hand. See Figure 138.

Repeat this for the second step. On your second step back with your right foot, however, you prolong it by taking it back beyond your left and out to the side, to point diagonally at an angle of 45 degrees towards your partner, so that when he advances his right for the third time you will be in a position to put your left sole in the way and throw him with the propping drawing ankle throw (Sasae Tsurikomi Ashi), as

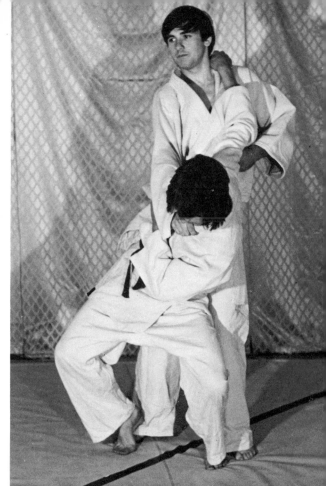

NAGE NO KATA

described in Set One, no. 3, of The Gokyo. See Figure 139.

When he gets up, you follow him to the other end of the kata, throw on the opposite side, and so get back to your right ends of the kata axis.

3. *Uchi Mata*

Advance together until you meet in the centre of the kata axis. Take the normal holds, but with your right hand a little higher on his left lapel.

As the steps are apt to sound complicated, it will be simpler if you first think of the effect you are aiming at. You are going to take six small steps, beginning with the left foot, all forwards, but slightly turning all the time to your right, so that on your fifth you are facing your own end of the kata axis and ready to throw with your right foot against his left inner thigh. In the process of this stepping, you will have described an about-turn. Your partner, on the other hand, is going to take very large steps around the outside of you, beginning with his left, so that he goes completely round you and is facing the same way at the end as he was at the beginning. He has, in other words, simply moved around you in a circle.

It is done in this way. Pull him with your right hand on his left upper lapel, to make him take

his first big step with his left. At the same time take your first small step with your left, partly turning. See Figure 140.

Now move your right foot up to your left, as he brings his right up to his left.

Again, pull with your right hand as you take your third step, which is a little one forwards with your left. His third is a big one around you with his left. Again, your fourth is to close up your right and his fourth is to close up his right.

Your fifth step with your left, and his large fifth round you, put you both in such a position that when he takes his sixth, you do not take it but use your right leg to sweep the inner side of his left thigh, throwing him with the inner thigh throw (Uchi Mata), as described in Set Two, no. 8, of The Gokyo. See Figure 141.

He rises where he is, facing towards his end of the kata axis, and you, of course, are facing yours. You repeat the throw on the other side by reversing all directions and this brings you both back to your own ends of the kata.

As this is the end of a set, you again turn your backs to each other, pause, adjust your jackets, and turn back to face each other.

SET FOUR (SACRIFICE THROWS FALLING ON YOUR BACK)

1. *Tomoe Nage*

Advance together until you meet in the centre of the kata. Take the normal holds.

You push your partner backwards by walking forwards normally, beginning with your right foot. He retreats from your push, walking normally and starting by taking his left foot back.

On your fourth step forwards, which will be with your left, you put it deeply in between his legs, fall on your back, and bring your right foot up into his stomach for the stomach throw (Tomoe Nage), as described in Set Three, no. 7, of The Gokyo. See Figure 142.

It will be noted that he has retreated first on his left, then his right, so that his fourth step back would be with his right. For his fifth, he immediately brings his right forwards again to your left side, so that he can do the right rolling breakfall over you.

As you go down to perform the stomach throw it is considered better to change your left-hand hold on his sleeve to one on his right lapel that corresponds with your right hand hold on his left lapel.

When he is thrown, he does not remain on the ground but uses the impetus of his roll to come straight back up onto his feet. See Figure 143.

You get up facing him. He turns round. You come to the centre of the kata axis again and repeat on the other side.

2. Ura Nage

This is a throw for countering an attempt by your partner to strike you on top of the head with the bottom of his fist, as in Seoi Nage.

You come to a distance of six feet from him, he advances his left foot and swings back his right arm for the strike. You move your head to your right so that the blow passes over your left shoulder, step in with your left foot behind him, catch him around the back at belt level with your left arm and put your right hand in his stomach, your right elbow resting on your right hip. See Figure 144.

You are now in a position to do Ura Nage (the rear throw), as described in Set Five, no. 6, of The Gokyo. Lift him clear of the ground, fall on your back and throw him over your left shoulder. He does the right forwards rolling breakfall and lies where he has fallen. See Figure 145.

Repeat from the opposite ends of the kata axis on the other side, to bring you back to your own ends of the kata.

3. Sumi Gaeshi

You advance to normal holding distance and then both of you assume a deep crouching stance, legs wide apart, knees bent. Your left hand and his left take normal holds on the sleeves. But each of you thrusts his right under the other's left armpit, to hold around the back.

Your first step is to retreat with your left foot. Your partner follows with his right. See Figure 146.

You then take your right foot back, and he follows with his left.

For your third step, you take your left foot in to a point midway between his legs as he advances his right foot. You fall on your back and put your right instep against the inside of his left knee, so that you are in a position to throw him with the corner throw (Sumi Gaeshi), as described in Set Four, no. 1, of The Gokyo. See Figure 147.

He lands with a right forwards rolling breakfall and remains lying. You then get up together, go to the other end of the kata axis, repeat on the other side, and so get back to your normal ends.

This is the end of the fourth set, so again you go to your respective ends, turn your backs to each other, adjust your jackets, pause, and turn to face each other.

SET FIVE (SACRIFICE THROWS FALLING ON YOUR SIDE)

1. Yoko Gake

This is one of the three-step throws. Come in to normal distance, take the normal holds, and move backwards with your left, your partner following with his right. On the first steps you turn him slightly to his left by pushing his right sleeve across his body. See Figure 148.

On your second step back with your left foot you turn him a little more. See Figure 149.

On your third step, you do not actually take the step but apply your left foot to his outer right ankle and fall, pulling down with your left hand and turning him with your right onto his back in the side body drop (Yoko Gake) as described in Set Five, no. 8, of The Gokyo. See Figure 150.

Repeat on the opposite side, so returning to your own ends of the kata.

2. Yoko Guruma

The start of this is almost exactly as for Ura Nage (Set Four, no. 2, of this kata). But when

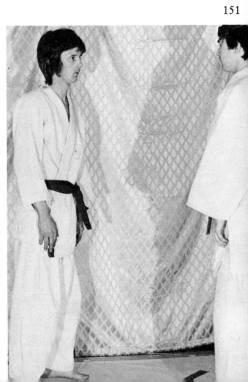

NAGE NO KATA

you come up to him, you both move to a position facing each other across the line of the kata, he with his back to the joseki, you facing it. You should make this move in two steps, left right, and simultaneously. You are at a distance of six feet. See Figure 151.

He now steps forwards with his left foot and goes to strike you with his right hand, as in Ura Nage. You dodge the blow and move in to where you can pick him up for Ura Nage. See Figure 152.

To avoid your Ura Nage, your partner now bends his body directly forwards to the front. You come around him and slide your right leg between his legs, pulling with your left hand and pushing with your right, so as to throw him with the side wheel (Yoko Guruma) as described in Set Five, no. 4, of The Gokyo. See Figure 153.

After doing his right forwards rolling break-fall he lies where he has fallen for a few moments and you then get up together. You go to the other end of the kata, take position across the axis of the kata and repeat on the other side. This brings you to your own end of the kata again.

15

3. Uki Waza

This is a throw from the crouching posture, like Sumi Gaeshi.

Come in to normal holding distance, and take up the deep crouch, knees bent, legs wide apart. Each of you keeps the same hold with left hand on the sleeve, but with your right you catch your opponent behind and under his left armpit. See Figure 154.

You step back with your left foot, he follows with his right. You step back with your right, he follows with his left.

152

1.

155

Now stretch your left foot widely to your left side and fall on your left side, your right foot on the ground. Let him disengage his right arm from your left hold on his sleeve, so that he can use it to breakfall. Throw him with the floating throw (Uki Waza) as described in Set Five, no. 2, of The Gokyo. See Figure 155.

He remains where he has fallen until you both get up together, go to the opposite ends of the kata, and repeat on the opposite side. You are now at the right ends of the kata. You turn your backs on each other and adjust your jackets. This is not only the end of the set but also the end of the kata and your attire must be impeccably arranged for the bow.

When you have turned to face each other, you both step back, right, left, so that your heels are brought together.

You make the standing bow to each other. Then, turning to face the joseki, you make the standing bow to the distinguished guests.

It should again be emphasised that every single detail must be correct in this sequence of movements. The slightest unnecessary movement, wrong turn or extra step, would count as a fault. And probably every black belt in the audience would notice those faults. Such perfection comes only with long practice between partners who have learnt to work in complete harmony.

CHAPTER EIGHT
Katame No Kata

Katame No Kata is the formal demonstration of groundwork movements. Again, it was created by Professor Jigoro Kano from a study of the ancient movements and dates from his day.

The techniques in this kata are grouped into three sets of five movements in each set. The first set consists of holdings (Osaekomi Waza); the second set of strangleholds (Shime Waza); and the third set of four armlocks and one leglock (Kansetsu Waza).

As with Nage No Kata, every detail must be accurate and there must be no unnecessary movement. The entire procedure is performed with dignity and respect.

The man who does the movements is again called Tori; the one to whom it is done is called Uke.

Tori and Uke will again take up the positions, about twelve feet apart, Tori to the left of the joseki and Uke to the right, as viewed from the joseki. They will stand silent, still and respectful for a moment, before simultaneously making the thirty degree turn to face the joseki, and to bow. See Figure 156.

They step forwards a pace left, right, to open their feet, then take up the high kneeling position (Tate Kyoshi No Kamae). To do this, they kneel on the left knee and turn the right foot to point outwards. See Figure 157.

Note that in this high kneeling position the toes of the left foot are dug into the mat. This is always the case in a fighting position and it is only when bowing that the toes are stretched out and the insteps are in contact with the mat. The right hand rests on the right knee.

From the high kneeling position, each will drop onto his right knee, stretch his toes out and, crossing the big toes, make the kneeling salutation as described in Chapter 1. See Figure 158.

Having made the bow, they return to the high kneeling position.

Now we come to the kata movements. You are Tori; your partner is Uke. Imagine, again, a straight line between you. This is the axis of the kata. Your partner must always lie along the axis for your demonstration.

To get down, he places both hands on the ground in front of him, takes his right foot under his arms, between them and his left knee which is on the mat, and so turns onto his back. He then lies flat along the axis of the kata, left knee up with the foot on the floor, right leg extended. See Figure 159.

Whilst he is doing this, you remain in the high kneeling position. All is now ready for the first demonstration.

SET ONE (HOLDINGS)

1. *Kesa Gatame*

Stand up. Turn to your right. Take three steps. Turn left ninety degrees and walk down to your partner's side, but three paces away from him. Turn to face him and drop into the high kneeling position. See Figure 160.

Advance on your left knee and right foot the three paces that bring you to his side. This is a difficult movement and can only be done with practice. When you reach him, pick up his right arm with your left holding his outer sleeve and your right his inner sleeve. See Figure 161.

Put your right knee under his right armpit and his right arm under your left, trapping it there, and drop into the scarf hold (Kesa Gatame), as described in the chapter on holdings (Chapter 4, no. 1). When you take this holding

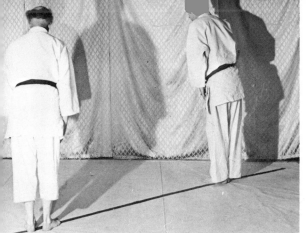

156   157

158   159

in your kata form, your right hand passes under his left armpit and holds his left shoulder to the ground. When you have taken up this position, be definitely seen to relax on him, so that he and the audience know you have got it. See Figure 162.

He will then try to get away by grasping your belt with his left hand and bridging, trying to buck you off over his left shoulder. This manoeuvre fails and he submits by tapping with his left hand.

2. *Kata Gatame*

Kneel at his side in the high kneeling position, without going out. Pick up his right wrist in your right hand and, by pushing on the elbow with your left, take it across his throat. See Figure 163.

Pass your right arm under his neck from his left side, catch the hand in your left, thrust your right knee under his right armpit, extend your left leg, and drop into the shoulder hold (Kata Gatame) as described in Chapter 4, no. 2. See Figure 164.

He will try to get away, first by bridging and trying to turn to his left, then by trying to push his right arm against the side of your neck with his left and so create a gap. Each time, you tighten your hold so that he is forced to submit by tapping with his left hand.

3. *Kami Shiho Gatame*

Take the high kneeling position at his side. Retreat the three steps on your left knee and right foot. Stand up. Turn at right angles to your left. Walk parallel to and as far as the end of the axis of the kata. Turn right and take the three steps that bring you directly behind your partner. Drop into the high kneeling position there. See Figure 165.

Advance on your left knee and right foot until you are directly behind his head in the high kneeling position. Ideally, you should do this in three steps. See Figure 166.

Pass both your hands under his shoulders and grasp his belt on either side. Put your right cheek on his stomach. Lower yourself on your right knee and spread your knees apart. Relax on him in the upper four quarters hold (Kami Shiho Gatame) as described in Chapter 4, no. 4). See Figure 167.

77

160

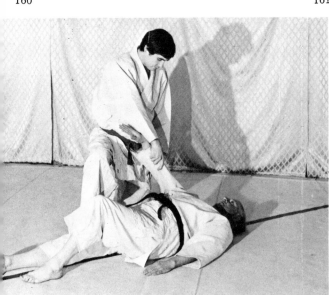

KATAME NO KATA

He will catch your belt with both hands and bridge, trying to turn to left and to right, but it will be in vain. He will submit by tapping with his left hand.

4. *Yoko Shiho Gatame*

Return to the high kneeling position directly behind your partner's head. Go back on left knee and right foot to your end of the kata axis. Stand up and turn to your right; take three steps, turn left, walk down to the side of your partner, turn to face him and drop into the high kneeling position, but three paces away as for the first movement. See Figure 168.

Approach to his side, with the three steps on left knee and right foot. Pick up his left knee in your left hand and thrust your right arm between his legs. See Figure 169.

Grasp his belt with your right hand. Pass your left under his head from his right side and hold his left shoulder to the ground. Drop into the side four quarters hold as described in Chapter 4, no. 3. See Figure 170.

He has his right hand under your stomach and with his left he catches your belt at the back in an attempt to swing you off. On failing to do so, he submits by tapping.

Take the high kneeling position at his side. Go back three steps on left knee and right foot. Stand up, turn left and go back to the end of the kata axis; turn right and go in the three steps that will take you directly behind your partner; face him and take the high kneeling position.

5. *Kuzure Kami Shiho Gatame*

Approach with the three steps on left knee and right foot until you are directly behind his head. Pick up his right arm in your left and pass it under your right. With your right hand catch his collar at the back of his neck. Do all this slowly, so that your precise actions can be clearly seen. See Figure 171.

Put your left arm under his left shoulder, catch his belt, and pull him to the ground. Drop onto your right knee and spread your knees. Put your right cheek on his stomach and lower yourself into the broken upper four quarters (Kuzure Kami Shiho Gatame), as described in Chapter 4, no. 5). See Figure 172.

He catches your belt with his left hand and tries to roll you to the left but, on failing, submits by tapping.

KATAME NO KATA

You take up the high kneeling position, retreat on left knee and right foot to your end of the kata axis and, since it is the end of a set, you wait there.

He gets up in exactly the opposite way to that in which he got down, ie, by rolling to his right, putting both hands on the ground, bringing his right leg between his hands and his left, and rising to the high kneeling position.

You are both facing each other now in the high kneeling position at your respective ends of the kata axis. You pause to adjust your jackets in readiness for the next set.

SET TWO (STRANGLEHOLDS)

1. *Kata Juji Jime*

He gets down onto his back, exactly as before. You stand up, take three steps to your right, turn and walk to his right side, but three paces away, drop into the high kneeling position and approach those three paces on left knee and right foot, exactly as before. You are now in the high kneeling position at his right side.

Pick up his right arm in both your hands and lay it on the ground at right angles to his body. Slide your left knee in to make the closest possible contact with his right side. Now swing your right leg across him, spreading his left arm out at right angles to his body as you do so by pushing it with your right hand from under the elbow joint. Kneel astride him. See Figure 173.

With your left hand, grasp his left lapel, thumb inside, fingers out, and apply the bony edge of your left forearm (little finger edge) against his throat. With your right hand catch his right lapel and pull down. You are now applying the half cross (Kata Juji Jime) on the opposite side to that described in Chapter 6, no. 3. See Figure 174.

He tries to bend forwards to stop the strangulation, but you take your head to the ground over his right shoulder and he will submit by tapping.

You come back to the high kneeling position astride him and retreat down his legs by steps, moving on your left knee and right foot. When you are clear of his body, you stand up, turn left, walk three paces, then turn right and walk parallel to the axis of the kata to your own end.

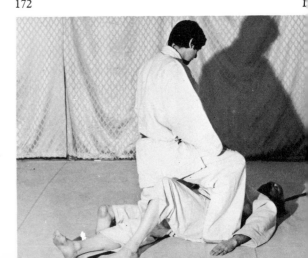

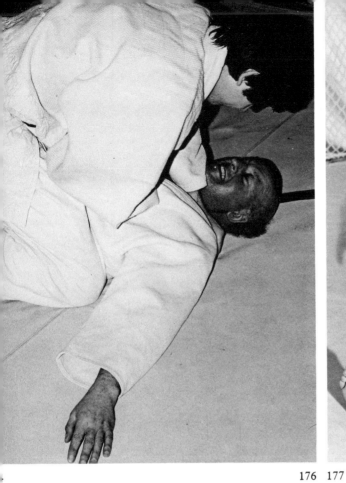

175

You then turn right and walk three paces, finally turning to face your partner and dropping into the high kneeling position.

He now sits up, with his left knee up and his right leg extended. You approach him on left knee and right foot until you are close behind him. Ideally, this should be done in three steps.

2. *Hadaka Jime*

Pass your right arm over his right shoulder and across the front of his throat, the bony edge of the thumb side against his throat. Put the palm in the crook of your left elbow and your left palm against the back of his neck. Retreat your left knee half a pace to bring him off balance backwards, and you can then apply the necklock from rear, as described in Chapter 6, no. 8. See Figure 175.

Sometimes the naked necklock (Ushiro Jime) as described in Chapter 6, no. 7, is applied instead.

In either case he tries to relieve pressure by seizing your right sleeve with both hands and pulling forwards and downwards. It is ineffective, and he submits by tapping.

3. *Okuri Eri*

Let him go, but stay in the same position. Bring your left knee back the half pace. Pull his left lapel down with your left hand, your left arm going under his left armpit. Pass your right hand over his right shoulder and catch his left lapel well up behind his ear. See Figure 176.

Now pass your left arm under his left armpit and catch his right lapel. Pull it down as you take your right elbow back. Retreat the half pace on your left knee to take him off balance backwards and you are applying the sliding collar (Okuri Eri), as described in Chapter 6, no. 5. See Figure 177.

He will try to escape by pulling your right sleeve with both hands, but when it fails he will submit by tapping. Bring your left knee back the half pace, let him go, and remain where you are.

4. *Kata Ha Jime*

Again you pass your left arm under his left armpit and pull his left lapel down. You pass your right arm over his right shoulder and catch his left lapel well back behind his ear, just as though you were going to repeat Okuri Eri. At this point he raises his left arm and tries to seize your head. See Figure 178.

Instantly, slide your left arm across the back of his neck and take the half pace back with your left knee to unbalance him. This is the single wing necklock (Kata Ha Jime), as described in Chapter 6, no. 6. See Figure 179.

He tries to escape by pulling your right sleeve with his right hand, but it is unsuccessful and when he submits you let him go.

You now retreat three paces on left knee and right foot to your position at the end of the kata axis. He lies on his back, left knee up, right foot extended. You rise, turn right, take three steps, turn left, and walk to the side of your partner, standing three paces away from him. You then turn to face him and drop into the high kneeling position.

5. *Gyaku Juji Jime*

Approach the three steps on left knee and right foot. Pick up his right arm in both yours and place it at right angles to his body. Bring your left knee close against his right side. Swing your right leg across him and kneel, spreading his left arm as you do so, all just as in the first movement of this set.

You are now kneeling astride him, knees close to his sides. Cross your arms and catch his collar on either side, fingers in, thumbs out, and apply the reverse cross (Gyaku Juji Jime) as described in Chapter 6, no. 2. See Figure 180.

If your right arm is over your left, he applies his left hand to your right elbow and his right hand to your left, and rolls you over to his right. You go with him, bringing him with you so that you are underneath. Apply your feet to his body, just under the hips, as you continue to strangle in the lateral cross (Yoko Juji Jime), as described in Chapter 6, no. 4. See Figure 181.

He will submit. Roll him back over to the original position, with you astride him. Move down his body on left knee and right foot until you are clear of him. Stand up, turn left, and take three paces. Turn right and walk parallel to the axis of the kata to your own end. Turn right and move in the three steps that take you directly behind him. Turn to face him and kneel in the high kneeling position. Wait there.

As this is the end of the set, he also gets up to the high kneeling position, exactly as previously described. You adjust your jackets and there is a pause to indicate the end of a set.

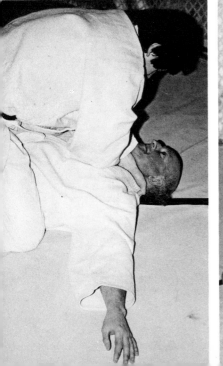

KATAME NO KATA

He gets down onto his back as before.

1. Ude Garami

You rise and, as in the first move, come to his right side in the high kneeling position.

He reaches up his left arm, intending to grab your right lapel. See Figure 182.

Catch his left wrist with your left hand and take it to the floor, his upper arm being out at right angles to his body and his forearm bent back towards his head. Drop onto your right knee, lie across him, and pass your right arm under his left upper arm to grasp your own left wrist, with fingers uppermost. Bend both wrists to the ground and you will be doing the entangled armlock (Ude Garami) as described in Chapter 5, no. 2. See Figure 183.

Extend your right leg and keep your left knee up against him. He will try to raise his stomach and bend back to relieve the pressure, but your weight will hold him down and he will give in by tapping.

Return to the high kneeling position at his right side, without going out.

2. Ude Hishigi Juji Gatame

He puts his left arm back beside his body, and this time he raises his right arm to try and grasp your left lapel. See Figure 184.

You will see that by this move he is turning his elbow joint towards you. Catch his wrist with both hands, put your right shin close against his right side, lift your left leg and take it across his throat, putting the foot on the ground the other side of him, and fall back. Keep your knees together, hold his wrist to your chest and slightly raise your stomach. You will be doing the cross armlock (Juji Gatame) in the third variation of it, as described in Chapter 5, no. 1. See Figure 185.

He arches his body and tries to bend back to relieve pressure, but it is useless and he taps in surrender with his left hand.

Return to the high kneeling position at his right side, without going out.

3. Ude Hishigi Ude Gatame

With both hands, move his right arm to your left side, that is out at right angles to his body. He now turns slightly on his right side and reaches up with his left arm to try and grasp your right lapel. See Figure 186.

182

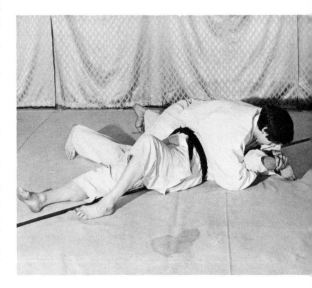

184

Press your right knee against his left side. Clasp your hands over his elbow joint, turning it away from your body, and pull the joint in towards your chest. Press down on his wrist with your right shoulder. You will be doing the arm crush (Ude Gatame) as described in Chapter 5, no. 3. See Figure 187.

He will give in without a struggle, and indicate this by tapping. Take up the high kneeling position at his side and from there back out as normally, stand up and return as usual to your end of the kata axis. Take the high kneeling position and he will get up to the same position as if the kata had ended.

4. Ude Hishigi Hiza Gatame

Approach each other on left knee and right foot until you are near enough to take the normal holds on each other, ie, on sleeve and lapel, as if you were standing up. See Figure 188.

Let go his right sleeve with your left hand and, putting your arm over his wrist and your hand under his arm, grasp the upper part of his sleeve from above. The effect of this is to trap his right wrist under your left armpit. Apply your right foot to his left thigh, on which he is kneeling. See Figure 189.

Push with your right foot to take him down, turn on your right side and bring your left knee up onto his right elbow joint so that you can apply the knee armlock (Hiza Gatame) as described in Chapter 5, no. 4. See Figure 190.

He taps with his foot to give in.

5. Ashi Garami

After his submission, take the high kneeling position and he will do the same. You both then retreat on left knee and right foot until you are six feet apart. Then you both stand up. Move close enough to take the normal holds, beginning with the left foot.

You now slide your left foot between his legs, raise your right leg and put it in his stomach, as though you were going to perform the stomach throw (Tomoe Nage). See Figure 191.

To avoid this move, he will step well forwards with his right leg, to your left side. Take your left leg around this from the outside and put your left foot in his right groin. See Figure 192.

Now, with your right leg push his left away at the knee so that he falls onto his left knee. Push your left strongly through in front of his

185

186

187

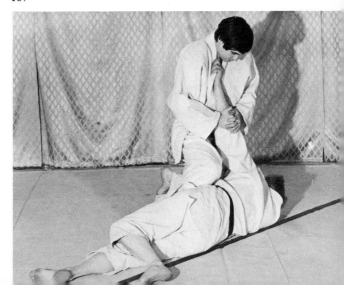

188

189

abdomen and you will have a painful lock on his right leg. See Figure 193.

He will tap in surrender and you let him go.

Take the high kneeling position, as at the beginning of the kata. Drop onto your right knees together and make the kneeling bow to each other. Rise and, turning simultaneously to the joseki, make the standing bow.

This concludes the kata.

It should be emphasised that the leg lock just described is absolutely banned in competition or in randori.

190

192

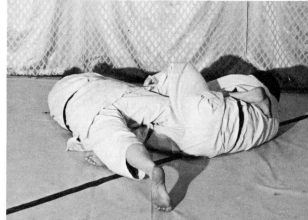

CHAPTER NINE
Kime No Kata

Kime No Kata is a kata of self-defence movements. It is sometimes called Shinken Shobu No Kata, or forms of real fighting. There are two divisions. The first set consists of eight movements and is called Idori. These are all performed in a kneeling position. The second set is called Tachiai and consists of twelve movements performed in a standing position.

Some of the movements use the sword, which is the long samurai two-handed sword. Others use the dagger, a shorter and more personal weapon. Before practising with either of these weapons, which are razor sharp, learn the movements thoroughly with imitation weapons. For when the kata has been mastered and is performed in earnest the attacks must be real and you must be able to get out of the way.

Tori is on the left of the joseki and Uke on the right as before, as viewed from the joseki. Uke holds the two weapons in his right hand at this stage. He will transfer them to his left side only when he is going to use them. He holds the dagger on top, the sword underneath, with the guards in front and on top, the points behind him and hanging down.

They begin twelve feet apart, with the usual standing salutation to the joseki. See Figure 194.

They then take the high kneeling position as described in the last chapter and Uke lays down his weapons by his right side, parallel to the axis of the kata, with the guards to the front and the points behind him. The sword is laid on the outside, the dagger on the inside. The curve of the blade is in towards him. They then lower their right knees simultaneously and make the formal kneeling bow to each other. See Figure 195.

They now resume the high kneeling position and while Tori retains this, Uke picks up his weapons in his right hand, stands up, turns about, goes to the end of the kata axis, kneels and lays down his sword and dagger. Note that when he kneels to do this, as when he bows, his toes are extended and not dug into the mat. See Figure 196.

Again the sword is placed outside at right angles to the axis of the kata, and the dagger inside with the guards towards the joseki and the points away from it. Again, the curve of the blade is towards Uke.

Having ceremoniously laid his weapons down, Uke takes the high kneeling position and both he and Tori then rise together. He turns to face Tori and they advance until they are about three feet apart. Then both assume first the high kneeling position, then the kneeling position, on both knees. Their toes are still extended at this point. Both place their clenched fists on the ground, just inside their knees and, taking support on these, they advance on their knees until they are about six inches apart. See Figure 197.

They are now in position for the first set of movements, Idori.

A word should perhaps be said here about this seated position, as it appears rather artificial to western eyes. It was the normal seated position of the Japanese in older days when houses did not have chairs and people sat on cushions on the floor. It would therefore be as natural a posture as sitting in a chair to a Westerner. Practice of it, as in this kata, strengthens the ankle joints and makes them more supple, so that it is a beneficial exercise in itself.

There should be a brief pause at this moment, and the two partners should take a few deep breaths to concentrate their attention on what they are about to do.

KIME NO KATA

From this point on we will again assume that you are Tori (the man who does the demonstration), and your partner is Uke (the one to whom it is done). However, in this kata Uke is going to take the initiative every time and your action will be the response to his attack on you.

SET ONE (ATTACKS IN KNEELING POSITION)

1. *Ryote Dori* (Wrists Held with Both Hands)

Your partner comes up onto his toes, toes dug into the mat, and seizes your right wrist in his left hand and your left wrist in his right hand. See Figure 198.

You take support on your left knee, dig your left toes into the mat, part your arms slightly so as to disturb his balance forwards and, raising the right foot bent at the knee, you deliver a kick to his solar plexus with the ball of your right foot. This is one of the atemi-waza, or blows at vital points of the old ju-jitsu schools. Be careful, of course, not to actually land it in the demonstration but to stop just short of the target. See Figure 199.

The kick is accompanied by what is called the 'kiai'. This is a shout, emanating from the lower abdomen which could startle an opponent who was not expecting it. It is really a sharp expulsion of breath and concentrates the force of your counter-attack, rather as karate men shout when they strike. The actual sound is 'Ee-itt' and this shout accompanies each counter-attack in this kata.

Having delivered the kick, you replace your right knee on the floor with toes dug into the mat, rise on your left foot and turn to your left. You free your left hand from your partner's grip by pulling it out against his thumb, which is the weakest point. Catch his left wrist with both hands and pull his arm straight, trapping it under your right arm. Bear down on his elbow joint with your right upper arm and shoulder. This is a variant of the straight armlock. See Figure 200.

Your partner will submit by tapping with his right hand. Return to the kneeling position with toes extended, but about a foot apart.

2. *Tsuki Kake* (Stomach Punch)

Your partner comes up onto his toes, toes dug into the mat, raises his body and tries to punch you in the solar plexus with a straight right-hand

194

196

202

204

punch. To avoid the punch, you pivot on your left knee, digging your toes in and raising your hips, and take your right foot back around behind you, so that you are facing parallel to the axis of the kata. This takes you out of the way of the punch as it is following the axis line of the kata and your turn has placed you just behind this line. As you do this, you come up on the right foot, right knee raised.

Now, as you are doing this turn, you must catch your partner's right wrist with your left hand, the fingers towards you, the thumb the other side, and with your right fist strike him between the eyes. Your left-hand pull on his wrist forwards and the impetus of his own punch are pulling him onto this punch of yours, which is delivered to the accompaniment of the kiai. See Figure 201.

Be very careful, however, not to land the blow, for it is one that can kill.

Having launched the blow, catch his right wrist with your right hand from above in a normal grip and continue pulling the arm across your body. Put your left hand over his left shoulder and catch his right lapel, as deeply in as possible. Straighten up and push your stomach forwards against his right elbow. This is a straight armlock in which the pressure is applied with your stomach, and it is called 'Haragatame'. At the same time, of course, you are strangling him with his right lapel pulled back against his throat by your left hand. See Figure 202.

This stomach armlock features in many of the defences, so practise it well. Your partner will submit by tapping.

Return to the formal kneeling posture, as at the beginning of the movement.

3. *Suri-Age* (Thrust at the Forehead)

Your partner rises onto his toes, toes dug into the mat, and tries to strike a blow at your forehead with the heel of his hand. His fingers are together and the blow is what is known in karate as the palm heel strike (teisho). It could alternatively be at the chin or under the base of the nose, and some masters teach each of these variations. The object is to jerk your head back and dislocate your neck. Slightly bend your body backwards so that the blow would pass you, come up onto your toes and raise your hips. See Figure 203.

Raise your hands. With the palm of your right hand ward off his blow by catching his wrist and with your left hand catch his right armpit with a normal hold, fingers at the back of him, thumb under the armpit. Kick him in the solar plexus with the ball of your right foot, accompanied by the kiai. See Figure 204.

Having delivered the kick, bring your right foot back and widely round behind you. Stretch out his right arm, bringing him onto his face. Keep your left knee close to his body and hold his right shoulder down with your left hand. Once you have control of him, kneel on his right elbow joint with your left knee. Do this very carefully in the demonstration, otherwise you will dislocate the joint before he has time to give in. See Figure 205.

He submits. Return to the formal kneeling position as at the beginning of this movement.

4. *Yoko Uchi* (Blow at the Temple)

This again, is one of the atemi blows taken over by karate. Your partner comes up on his toes as before, raising his hips, and tries to strike a blow at your left temple with the bottom of his right fist. See Figure 206.

To avoid this, come up on the toes of your left foot, bring your right foot, knee up, in close to the outside of his right knee, and duck your head under his right armpit. With your right hand push his left shoulder, your own right shoulder being against his right. With your left hand push in the left lower region of his back. See Figure 207.

From this position you can take him over onto his back and have him in the shoulder hold (Kata Gatame) position as described in Chapter 4, no. 2. See Figure 208.

Now block his right arm across his throat by pushing on the elbow with your left, and with your right elbow strike him a blow in the solar plexus, accompanying it with the kiai. See Figure 209.

Return to the formal kneeling position.

5. *Ushiro Dori* (Shoulder Seizure from behind)

Your partner rises, walks round behind you and kneels close to your body. He raises his right knee, comes up on his left toes, and attempts to encircle your shoulders with his arms. His head is kept close to the right side of yours to prevent your hitting him in the face with a sudden backwards movement of your own head. See Figure 210.

Come up onto your toes. Seize his left arm with both yours, drive your right leg through his behind him, and throw him over your left shoulder with the shoulder throw by rolling to your left. See Figure 211.

Hold him down with your right arm across his body and with your left fist hit him in the testicles. But be careful not actually to land the blow, of course. See Figure 212.

The blow is accompanied, as usual, with the kiai. If the assailant were a woman, the blow would be aimed two inches below her navel, at the hypogastrium, or at one of her breasts.

You both now rise to your feet and your partner goes to the end of the kata axis where he has left his weapons. As he kneels down to pick one up, you kneel down simultaneously with him. He picks up the dagger and conceals it inside his jacket. See Figure 213.

6. *Tsuki Komi* (Thrust with Dagger at Stomach)

He returns and takes the formal kneeling position facing you, but about two feet away. The dagger is inside his left jacket so that he can pull it out with his right hand. He draws it and takes it back for the thrust. See Figure 214.

In making the thrust, he comes up on his left foot, raising the knee and stepping forwards, and rises on his right toes.

You raise your right knee, come onto your left toes, and take your body and right foot round to a position parallel with the axis of the kata so that the thrust, being directly down the axis of the kata, would pass just in front of you. The other movements are exactly as for the stomach punch (Tsuki Kake), as described in no. 2 of this series. You catch his right wrist with your left hand and deliver a blow between the eyes with your right fist. See Figure 215.

Be very careful not to catch too soon or you will grab the blade of the dagger, which would be disastrous. Let it go by you before you catch.

Having struck the blow, accompanied by the kiai, change hands. Catch his wrist with your right and continue pulling him forwards off balance. Take your left hand over his left shoulder and, grasping his right lapel as far in as you can, apply the stomach armlock and stranglehold combined. See Figure 216.

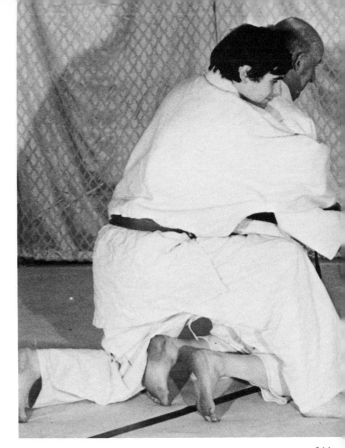

210 211

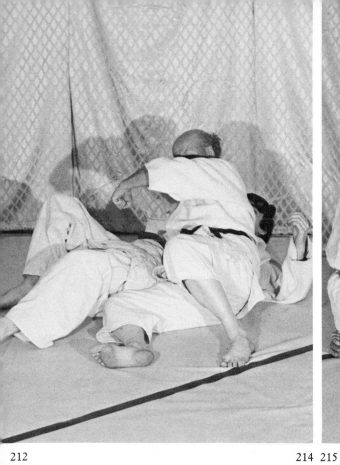

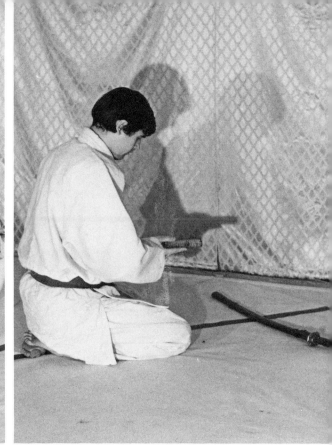

212

214 215

2

He will give in by tapping. You then return to the formal kneeling posture two feet apart and your opponent replaces the dagger in its sheath.

It should again be emphasised that all these dagger thrusts, and the sword movements which come later, must first be thoroughly practised with imitation weapons, for the real ones are highly dangerous.

7. *Kiri Komi* (Direct Down Cut at Head with Dagger).

Your partner unsheathes his dagger and raises it above his head to make a direct down cut at your head. See Figure 217.

In making the cut, he will come up on his left toes and this time raise his right knee. He will take a step forwards with his right foot as he strikes.

Come up onto your left toes, raise your right knee and make the usual turn to your right so that you are parallel to the axis of the kata and the cut passes down in front of you. Catch his right wrist with your right hand and pass your left arm over his right arm, imprisoning it under your left armpit. Pull him off balance, let your left hand join your right at his wrist and your left forearm press down on his elbow joint, so that you have an armlock on his right elbow joint. See Figure 218.

He will give in and replace the dagger in its sheath, whereupon you return to the original position.

8. *Yoko Tsuki* (Dagger Thrust from Side)

Your partner gets up and comes to your right side about eight inches away, kneels and unsheathes the dagger. He rises on his right toes, lifts his left knee and takes the dagger back, ready for the strike at your side. See Figure 219.

You have to do an about face turn to avoid this, raising your right knee and pivoting on your left. You will then be facing the other way round and parallel to the axis of his strike, which is at right angles to the axis of the kata.

As you complete the turn, catch his right wrist with your left hand and pull him forwards into a right-handed punch between the eyes. See Figure 220.

The punch is accompanied by the kiai. Change hands, catch his right wrist with your right, and pass your left hand over his left shoulder so as

216

217

218

219

220

221

to execute the combined stomach armlock and stranglehold, as in the stomach thrust described in no. 6 of this series. See Figure 221.

He will submit.

You now stand and keep perfectly still, facing the far end of the kata axis, while your partner takes the dagger there in its sheath, kneels and puts it down exactly where he picked it up. He will then rise and come to face you, standing about a foot away, ready for the next series.

SET TWO (ATTACKS IN THE STANDING POSITION)

1. *Ryote Dori* (Both Hands Seizure)

Your partner grabs both your wrists in the normal hold, thumbs inside, fingers out. See Figure 222.

Step backwards one pace with your left foot, spreading your arms to bring him off balance forwards. Kick him in the testicles with your right foot, using the ball of the foot and accompanying the kick with the kiai. This is what is known as a snap kick in karate. You raise the knee, deliver the kick, and bend the knee again before returning the foot to the mat. See Figure 223.

Free your left hand and, turning to your left, grab his left wrist with both your hands. You will find that, as you turn, your right will slide round in his grasp all right, enabling you to do this. Apply your right upper arm to the back of his left elbow and you will have a straight armlock on his left arm. See Figure 224.

He will tap in submission. You let him go and you both resume the upright posture, facing each other.

2. *Sode Tori* (Hold on Sleeve from Side)

He will now walk round to your left side and slightly behind you, and catch your left sleeve at the elbow as though to march you away. He holds it in his right hand. See Figure 225.

Take two steps forwards with each foot in turn, moving with Tsugi Ashi. Your partner follows. On the third step forwards with your right, use the side of your left foot, little toe edge, to deliver a kick at his right kneecap. This is a thrusting kick, known in karate as sokuto. It can dislocate the knee, so be careful not to land it. Accompany the kick with the kiai. See Figure 226.

222 224 225 223

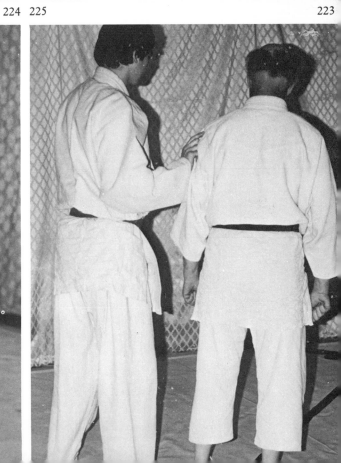

KIME NO KATA

Now, instantly bring your left foot back down, turning about face as you do so, grip his left lapel with your right hand and his right sleeve with your left. Then throw him backwards with O Soto Gari, as described in Set One, no. 5, of the Gokyo. See Figure 227.

3. *Tsuki Kake* (Straight Right to the Face)

You stand about nine feet apart. He brings his left foot forwards and takes his right fist back to strike you in the face. See Figure 228.

As he punches, he will bring his right foot forwards. Do a half turn to your right, by taking your right foot back and around so that you are parallel to the axis of the kata, and his punch will go by you. Deflect it still further with your right hand, catching the bottom of his right sleeve and pulling it forwards and downwards. Your left hand catches the upper part of his right sleeve. See Figure 229.

As he is being pulled off balance forwards, he will react by trying to straighten up. As he does so, let your right arm slide up his and step behind him with your left foot. Your right arm passes across the front of his throat, bony thumb edge of the arm against his throat. Your left hand passes over his left shoulder to catch your own right wrist and pull it back, and you unbalance him backwards to apply the naked necklock (Ushiro Jime) as described in Chapter 6, no. 7. This time, of course, you are doing it in the standing position instead of on the ground. See Figure 230.

He will give in, and indicate this by tapping.

4. *Tsuki Age* (Uppercut)

You stand about three feet apart. With his

right fist, your partner tries to give you an uppercut. Take your head back so that the fist passes in front of your chin and harmlessly up past it. See Figure 231.

Catch his right wrist with both hands, left just below right, and continue the upward movement of his arm until it is straight. See Figure 232.

Now turn by taking your right foot back and around, and bring his right arm under your left armpit. By bearing down on his elbow joint with your armpit and lifting his wrist, the little finger edge of his right arm uppermost you will apply a straight armlock against his right elbow joint. See Figure 233.

He will tap in submission.

5. *Suri Age* (Thrust at the Forehead)

You stand about three feet apart. With the palm of his right hand, your partner tries to thrust at your forehead in the same way as in the kneeling attack, no. 3 of the first series. Step back with your right foot and sway back slightly to avoid the blow, at the same time deflecting his attacking arm upwards with your left. See Figure 234.

Now, hit him with your right fist in his solar plexus. See Figure 235. Give the kiai shout.

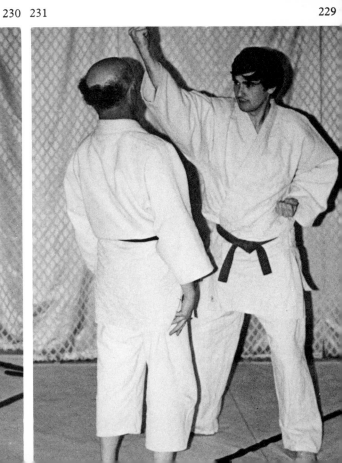

232. 234 235 23

36   238 239   237

Turn, by stepping through with your left foot, and throw him with the floating loin throw (Uki Goshi) applied to his left side. See Figure 236.

The throw is described on the more normal right-hand side in Set One, no. 4, of the Gokyo.

6. *Yoko Uchi* (Blow at Temple)

You stand about four feet apart. Your partner swings his right fist back with the intention of hitting you on the side of the temple. See Figure 237.

As he strikes he will advance his right foot. Sink your body, step to your left with your left foot and let the blow go over your right shoulder. As you do so, grasp his left lapel with your right hand, thumb inside. See Figure 238.

Step round behind him, pass your left hand over his left shoulder, catch his right lapel and apply the sliding collar (Okuri Eri) as described in Chapter 6, no. 5, except that this time you are doing it with the opposite hands. See Figure 239.

You must bring him off balance backwards as you apply the stranglehold, and you must move in very quickly indeed.

He will tap in submission.

7. *Ke Age* (Kick at the Testicles)

You stand about four feet apart and your partner tries to kick you in the testicles with his right foot. Turn your body by stepping back with your right foot, so that you are parallel to the axis of the kata, and the kick will go past you. See Figure 240.

Now, catch his ankle with both hands and take it to his right. Step back round to face him. See Figure 241.

Kick him in the testicles with your right foot, just as he was trying to do to you. See Figure 242.

Be careful not to land the kick, of course.

8. *Ushiro Dori* (Shoulder Seizure from Behind)

You stand in the normal position about three feet apart. Your partner then walks round behind you. You start to advance, but he comes up quickly and seizes you round the shoulders. See Figure 243.

The moment before he actually clasps his hands in front of you, drop onto your right knee, catch his right arm with both yours, and insert your right shoulder under his right armpit. See Figure 244.

You can now do the shoulder throw (Seoi

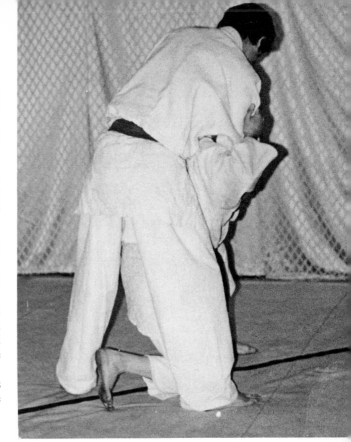

244

245

KIME NO KATA

Nage), as described in Set One, no. 8, of the Gokyo, with the variation that it is done from a kneeling position. See Figure 245.

When he has gone over, strike him between the eyes with the little finger edge of your right hand, controlling him with your hold on his right sleeve with your left hand. See Figure 246.

Accompany the blow with the kiai.

Stand perfectly still now, facing down the line of the kata to your partner's end as he goes there, kneels down and picks up his dagger. He then comes back to face you, standing about four feet away.

9. *Tsuki Komi* (Stomach Thrust with Dagger)

Your partner steps forward with his left foot and takes the dagger back to thrust it into your stomach. See Figure 247.

Step back and around with your right foot, turning so that the thrust goes past you, because you are parallel to the axis of the kata and the thrust is directly along the axis. Catch his right wrist with your left hand, pull forwards, and with your right hand deliver a punch between his eyes, accompanying it with the kiai. See Figure 248.

When making the thrust, he will, of course, have stepped forwards with his right foot. Now change hands. Hold his wrist with your right and pass your left over his left shoulder to obtain the combined stomach armlock and stranglehold as in the same attack from the kneeling position (no. 6 in the last series). See Figure 249.

247

24

246

10. *Kiri Komi* (Direct Down Cut at Head with Dagger)

You are about five feet apart. Your partner again unsheathes his dagger and, advancing his right foot, tries to cut directly down at your head. See Figure 250.

Take your right foot back and turn, so that being parallel to the axis of the kata the strike will pass down in front of your body. Take your left arm over his right arm, trapping it under your left armpit, and catch his right wrist with your right hand. See Figure 251.

Turn a little more and bear down on his elbow joint with your left armpit as you lift his wrist with both hands, being sure to get the little finger edge uppermost. You will have a straight armlock on his right elbow joint. See Figure 252.

He will give in, and indicate this by tapping.

Stand perfectly still, facing your partner's end of the kata. He will go and kneel down to replace his dagger. Then he will pick up his sword and, taking the high kneeling position, tie the sheath to his left belt with the string provided for that purpose. He will rise and come to face you at a distance of about six feet.

11. *Nuki Kake* (Sword Unsheathing)

Holding the top of the sheath with his left hand, he attempts to draw the sword with his right. See Figure 253.

As he does so, he advances his right foot. You advance your right foot to meet his, and with your right hand, fingers above and thumb below, you block his right wrist. See Figure 254.

250

Step behind him with your left foot. Pass your left hand over his left shoulder and catch his right collar as high up as you can. Now slide your right arm under his right armpit and up behind his neck, taking him off balance backwards as you do so. You will be applying the single wing necklock (Kata Ha Jime) as described in Chapter 6, no. 6, but of course you will be doing it from a standing position and with the opposite hands to the demonstration described in that chapter. See Figure 255.

He will tap in submission.

It should be noted that the sword is worn with the edge upwards.

12. *Kiri Oroshi* (Direct Down Cut at Head with Sword)

You are ten feet apart. Your partner unsheathes the sword. He can at this point either wear the sheath tied to his belt as before, or he can lay it on the ground at his left side. He takes a half pace forward with his right foot and holds the sword with both hands, right hand higher than the left. The point of the sword is directed upwards to the level of your eyes. See Figure 256.

This position is known as Chudan, the 'on guard' position in Japanese fencing. He then raises the sword above his head, steps forwards with left foot, then the right, and brings it down to cut directly down on your head. See Figure 257.

Step back with your right foot, turning your body so that, being parallel to the axis of the kata, the cut will pass down in front of your body. Catch his right wrist with your right hand after the sword passes and pull him forwards off

251

253 254

2

balance. Pass your left arm over his left shoulder and catch his right collar high up. You are then in a position to execute the stomach armlock combined with the stranglehold that we have met with before, in the stomach thrust with dagger (Tsuki Komi) as described in no. 9 of this series. See Figure 258.

He taps to signal his submission.

This being the end of the kata, he transfers the sword in its sheath to his right hand and walks to his end of the axis while you remain standing motionless at your end. He takes the high kneeling position facing away from you, kneels completely, picks up his dagger, also in his right hand, and holding it on top and the sword underneath, rises, first to the high kneeling position, then to his feet, and turns to face you.

Together you go down to the high kneeling position, then onto your knees, feet extended, big toes crossed. He lays down the weapons at

his right side, exactly as before. You both perform the kneeling salutation. See Figure 259.

As you rise together, he picks up his weapons, and you both turn to the joseki to make the standing bow.

This particular kata dates from the sixteenth century and the samurai swords used were made of steel, single edged, curved and tempered. Some of the best swords were produced between AD 900 and 1530, after which there came a peaceful period in Japanese history, and the art of sword making began to decline. In the modern period, from 1868 onwards, sword makers turned to ordinary blacksmith's work.

The older swords made by craftsmen can be distinguished from the modern machine-made sword in that the temper line, about half an inch from the cutting edge, is wavy on the hand-made ones and straight on the machine-made ones. The handle can be removed, and that part of the blade which extends inside the handle (the tang)

will be found to be engraved with the maker's marks. Possibly even a document will be enclosed there, giving the history of the sword.

Seven attacks only were made with the sword, six of them cuts. These six were directly down at the head, as in the last item of the kata; diagonally down at the neck on either side; at either wrist, to chop the hand off; and upwards on the left side through the ribs to the heart. The only thrust was to the throat, made with the point.

The dagger was used single-handed in the same way, but also to stab at the stomach. It was the dagger that would be used in the ritual suicide, known as seppukku.

One final point about the katas. They must be practised in the rôles of both Tori and Uke. Uke's part is just as difficult, if not more so, than Tori's and it is only by complete co-operation between the two partners that a perfect performance can be given.

Acknowledgments

The photographs in this book were taken by Mr Don Watkins.
The movements are being demonstrated by Mr Raymond Williams, Mr Paul Jordan and the author.

Index to Movements

BREAKFALLS